HAMLYN
ALL COLOUR
INDIAN
COOKBOOK

HAMLYN
ALL COLOUR
INDIAN
COOKBOOK

TED SMART

Front cover shows, left to right:
Kofta in yogurt (recipe 53), Chicken in apricots (recipe 97), Dhai bhindi (recipe 121).

Back cover shows, clockwise from top left:
Spiced chicken soup (recipe 1), Raita (recipe 193), Rice pudding (recipe 217),
Plain fried rice (recipe 173), Grilled spiced fish (recipe 21)

Illustrations by Gillie Newman

This edition published in 1992
by Reed Consumer Books Limited
for The Book People
Guardian House, Borough Road
Godalming, Surrey GU7 2AE

Reprinted 1993

Some of the recipes in this book originally appeared in *The Hamlyn All Colour
Oriental Cookbook*, published in 1989.

A catalogue record of this book is available
from the British Library

ISBN 1 85613 114 9

Produced by Mandarin Offset
Printed in Hong Kong

CONTENTS

USEFUL FACTS AND FIGURES

NOTES ON METRIFICATION

In this book quantities are given in metric and Imperial measures. Exact conversion from Imperial to metric measures does not usually give very convenient working quantities and so the metric measures have been rounded off into units of 25 grams. The table below shows the recommended equivalents.

Ounces	Approx g to nearest whole figure	Recommended conversion to nearest unit of 25	Ounces	Approx g to nearest whole figure	Recommended conversion to nearest unit of 25
1	28	25	9	255	250
2	57	50	10	283	275
3	85	75	11	312	300
4	113	100	12	340	350
5	142	150	13	368	375
6	170	175	14	396	400
7	198	200	15	425	425
8	227	225	16(1lb)	454	450

Note

When converting quantities over 16 oz first add the appropriate figures in the centre column, then adjust to the nearest unit of 25. As a general guide, 1kg (1000g) equals 2.2 lb or about 2 lb 3 oz. This method of conversion gives good results in nearly all cases, although in certain pastry and cake recipes a more accurate conversion is necessary to produce a balanced recipe.

Liquid measures

The millilitre has been used in this book and the following table gives a few examples.

Imperial	Approx ml to nearest whole figure	Recommended ml	Imperial	Approx ml to nearest whole figure	Recommended ml
1/4	142	150ml	1 pint	567	600 ml
1/2	238	300ml	1 1/2 pints	851	900 ml
3/4	425	450ml	1 3/4 pints	992	1000 ml (1 litre)

Spoon measures

All spoon measures given in this book are level unless otherwise stated.

Can sizes

At present, cans are marked with the exact (usually to the nearest whole number) metric equivalent of the Imperial weight of the contents, so we have followed this practice when giving can sizes.

Oven temperatures

The table below gives recommended equivalents.

	°C	°F	Gas Mark		°C	°F	Gas Mark
Very cool	110	225	1/4	Moderately hot	190	375	5
	120	250	1/2		200	400	6
Cool	140	275	1	Hot	220	425	7
	150	300	2		230	450	8
Moderate	160	325	3	Very Hot	240	475	9
	180	350	4				

NOTES FOR AMERICAN AND AUSTRALIAN USERS

In America the 8-fl oz measuring cup is used. In Australia metric measures are now used in conjunction with the standard 250-ml measuring cup. The Imperial pint, used in Britain and Australia, is 20 fl oz, while the American pint is 16 fl oz. It is important to remember that the Australian tablespoon differs from the British and American tablespoons; the table below gives a comparison. The British standard tablespoon, which has been used throughout this book, holds 17.7 ml, the American 14.2 ml, and the Australian 20 ml. A teaspoon holds approximately 5 ml in all three countries.

British	American	Australian
1 teaspoon	1 teaspoon	1 teaspoon
1 tablespoon	1 tablespoon	1 tablespoon
2 tablespoons	3 tablespoons	2 tablespoons
3 1/2 tablespoons	4 tablespoons	3 tablespoons
4 tablespoons	5 tablespoons	3 1/2 tablespoons

AN IMPERIAL/AMERICAN GUIDE TO SOLID AND LIQUID MEASURES

Imperial	American	Imperial	American
Solid measures		**Liquid measures**	
1 lb butter or		1/4 pint liquid	2/3 cup liquid
margarine	2 cups	1/2 pint	1 1/4 cups
1lb flour	4 cups	1/4 pint	2 cups
1 lb granulated or		1 pint	2 1/2 cups
caster sugar	2 cups	1 1/2 pints	3 1/4 cups
1 lb icing sugar	3 cups	2 pints	5 cups
8 oz rice	1 cup		(2 1/2 pints)

NOTE: WHEN MAKING ANY OF THE RECIPES IN THIS BOOK, ONLY FOLLOW ONE SET OF MEASURES AS THEY ARE NOT INTERCHANGEABLE.

INTRODUCTION

India is a very large country, with major variations in climate, religion, local produce and custom, factors reflected in the diverse regional ways of preparing and serving food. The country's geographical position also means that evidence of long-ago foreign influences can be detected in some Indian dishes. However, a common theme that runs throughout Indian cookery is the careful blending of spices in different combinations and quantities to achieve variations in flavour within a wide range of meat, fish, poultry, vegetable and pulse dishes.

Traditionally, an Indian meal consists of one or two meat, poultry or fish dishes, one or two vegetable dishes and a pulse dish, all served together with rice or bread, yoghurt, a salad and a selection of chutneys and relishes. The quantities given in this book reflect this way of serving food. The food is placed directly on a round metal tray known as a *thali*, from which guests help themselves to as little or as much as they want. Alternatively, only the rice, if served, chutneys and accompaniments are placed directly on the *thali*, and the main dishes are served in bowls called *katoris* arranged around the *thali*.

A good means of combining the Indian way of serving food with western tradition is to treat each person's plate as a *thali*, grouping helpings of various dishes around a central serving of rice. Or you can simply treat the tabletop like a *thali* on a grand scale.

Menu-planning with Indian food is a delight: just aim to serve an assortment of dishes that complement each other in terms of flavour, colour and texture, combining spicy dishes with cool, refreshing ones; dry curries with moister foods; and including a number of brightly coloured dishes and garnishes. Desserts are not usually served at the end of an Indian meal, but there is nothing to stop you serving Indian sweetmeats or desserts following a main savoury course if you want. Adaptability is a key word in Indian cookery: you can follow Indian custom to the letter, not serving rice and bread together and omitting a sweet course if you prefer, or you can serve the food in Western-style courses of starter, main dish and dessert.

Alcohol is one feature of the Western dining table that does not easily adapt to Indian food. Most wines are unsuitable to serve with Indian dishes as they often cause a burning sensation in the mouth. The best drinks to serve with Indian food are ice-cold mineral water, beer, lager or lassi (see Cook's Tip, recipe 141).

Each recipe in this book is illustrated with a colour photograph, and every one is accompanied by a Cook's Tip, which gives short cuts, dietary information, and explanations about ingredients – particularly unfamiliar ones. Sometimes alternatives to unusual ingredients are given, but in most cases they are readily available in Indian supermarkets and speciality shops. To assist those counting the calories, every recipe in the book details the number of calories contained in one helping of the dish. Each recipe gives details of preparation and cooking times, so you can see at a glance whether you have time to prepare a particular dish on the same day as you want so serve it, or whether it is better to plan ahead. Remember, however, that it is a good idea to make curries in advance so the flavours are given the opportunity to develop their full potential. If you do this you must be sure to reheat dishes thoroughly right through to avoid any risk of food poisoning.

Whether you want food for entertaining or family meals; for vegetarians or fish- and meat-eaters; for delicious snacks, sweetmeats and accompaniments or substantial main courses, this book contains a wealth of ideas for cooking and presenting food in the Indian way.

INGREDIENTS

The following are some of the ingredients commonly found in Indian cookery. Most are readily obtainable, and more unusual ones can be found in Indian supermarkets and specialist shops. Whole spices such as cinnamon sticks and whole cardamom pods are usually discarded before a dish is served.

ANISEED
Available fresh or ground. The seeds are used in sweet and hot chutneys and confectionery, and the powdered form imparts a subtle liquorice flavour to meat and vegetable dishes.

ASAFOETIDA (HING)
A strong-smelling resin available either in lumps or ground into powder. It is supposedly useful as an aid to digestion and there are a number of varieties, ranging in colour from light yellow to dark brown. Used in very small quantities.

BESSAN
This is a fine yellow flour made from ground chick peas or split peas. Sift it before use as it often forms hard lumps during storage. It is high in protein and low in gluten.

BLACHAN
A paste or block of strong-smelling, salty dried shrimp flavouring that should be kept in a tightly closed jar or box to prevent its aroma overwhelming the entire kitchen. It must be fried or roasted before use.

BLACK SALT
A distinctively flavoured rock salt with traces of sulphur in it. It can be used to flavour chutneys and snacks.

CARDAMOM
This is available in three different forms: whole (with the seeds in their pods), as seeds, or ground. The pods vary in colour from white to green to almost black. The whole pod is used to flavour rice, meat and vegetable dishes and is then discarded, and the ground variety is sprinkled on vegetables and in sweets.

CHILLI
Chilli peppers can be bought fresh, when they are green, yellow or red; or dried, when they vary in colour from orange-brown to bright red. The dried variety is also available in flaked or ground form. When handling any type of chilli, take care not to put your hands anywhere near your eyes or face because it causes a painful burning sensation. Wash your hands afterwards, too.

CINNAMON
This is the dried bark of the cinnamon shrub that has been peeled off, rolled into sticks and then dried. In addition to cinnamon sticks or quills, you can buy it in powdered form. It is a very useful spice, being used to flavour meat and vegetable dishes, seafood, pickles, puddings, cakes and stewed fruits.

CLOVES
These are dried flower buds of an evergreen of the myrtle family available as whole cloves or ground; whole cloves are used in rice dishes and meat curries, and ground ones with fruit dishes.

COCONUT MILK/CREAM
Coconut milk is not the juice found inside a coconut, but an infusion made with the flesh of fresh or desiccated coconut, used to flavour and thicken sweet and savoury dishes. See Cook's Tip (recipe 2) for details of how to make coconut cream and milk. You can also buy creamed coconut for convenience.

CORIANDER
One of the most common ingredients in Indian cookery, and one of the most fragrant. It is available in three forms: as a fresh herb, frequently used as a garnish or in chutneys; as whole seeds; or ground. It is used in curries, garam masala, and many vegetable, pulses and grain dishes. Keep a peppermill full of coriander seeds ready to provide freshly ground coriander.

CUMIN
Many varieties of this are available, in whole seed and ground forms. Black cumin is perhaps the best type available: its seeds are smaller and darker and have a strong but pleasant aroma. Cumin is invariably added to garam masala and curry powders and sometimes to meat curries, and the whole seeds are often used in chutneys and vegetable curries.

CURRY LEAVES
These are the aromatic leaves of the sweet Nim tree, and are available in green or dried form. Like bay leaves, they are used for flavouring while cooking and discarded before serving.

CURRY POWDER
This is a commercially prepared western adaptation of the Indian art of blending spices. It can be obtained in various strengths from mild to very hot, and some blends may contain about fifty different spices, often including the traditional ones of coriander, turmeric, cumin, fenugreek and chilli.

FENNEL
The pale yellowish-green, aniseed-flavoured seeds are commonly used in Indian cookery, especially after dry-roasting or flash-frying them before use. They can be used crushed, and are often chewed as an aid to digestion.

FENUGREEK
Available as whole seeds or in ground form, fenugreek is slightly bitter so take care not to overdo its use. It is used in its ground form in curry powders, and the whole yellow seeds are often used in vegetable curries. Dry-roasting or flash-frying the whole seeds for a few seconds before use makes the flavour more mellow.

GARAM MASALA
This is a mixture of spices that can be bought ready-blended, although Indian cooks prefer to make up their own as and when it is needed. The mixture usually includes black pepper, cumin, cinnamon, coriander and cloves. The flavour is

undoubtedly better if you grind the mix of spices yourself: see Cook's Tip, recipe 21, for one suggested blend.

GARLIC
This can be bought fresh, or as a purée, flakes, powder or salt, though fresh gives the best flavour to a wide variety of Indian dishes. Garlic tends to burn quite easily when fried, and the flavour can become bitter. For this reason, some people prefer to add it for only a couple of seconds after other ingredients such as onions have been fried.

GHEE
A commonly used cooking fat, particularly in southern India, ghee is a clarified butter. It is able to withstand higher temperatures without burning than butter and most cooking oils. It can be bought in cans, or you can make it yourself at home (see Cook's Tip, recipe 19).

GINGER
This rhizome is available in a number of forms: whole fresh, whole dried, powdered and whole preserved in syrup or crystallized. Fresh root ginger is peeled and grated, crushed, sliced or chopped, then added to rice and sweet dishes, and often to meat curries. Keep it in a plastic bag in the refrigerator, checking occasionally that cut ends do not develop mould.

LEMON GRASS
Available in fresh and ground forms, this imparts a subtle lemon flavour to any dish. One teaspoon of the powdered variety is equivalent to one fresh stalk of lemon grass. Bruise fresh lemon grass with the handle of a knife or in a pestle and mortar to release the full flavour.

LENGKUAS
Lengkuas is a pine-flavoured root that looks rather like fresh ginger. It is usually sold in powdered form, known as laos powder.

MANGO POWDER, DRIED
Fresh, unripe green mangoes are peeled, stoned, cut into thin slices and dried, then ground to a powder. This makes a convenient substitute for tamarind pulp and is used to add sharpness to curries and other dishes.

MUSTARD SEEDS
These are available whole in black, white and brown varieties. The black variety are used to flavour vegetable and pulse curries. Dry-roasting or flash-frying for a few seconds before use releases their full flavour.

NUTMEG
Nutmeg can be bought whole or ground, though freshly ground nutmeg has a far superior taste to its commercially prepared counterpart. It is useful when making curry sauces.

ONION SEEDS
These are collected from shoots produced by the onion. The black teardrop-shaped seeds are used to add flavour to vegetable curries and Indian breads.

PALM SUGAR
Also known as gula jawa and jula malaka, this is sold in thin blocks; ordinary brown sugar may be used as an alternative.

PANIR
A simple curd cheese used in Indian cookery. You can buy it or make your own (see Cook's Tip, recipe 230)

POPPY SEEDS
A useful storecupboard ingredient, poppy seeds add a crunchy texture and nutty flavour to savoury dishes, salads, breads and are useful in thickening curries.

PULSES
There are sixty varieties of pulse – the dried seeds of plants such as beans and peas – available in India, and they form an important part of the Indian diet. They include chick peas, whole peas, red and yellow lentils, black gram, kidney beans and pigeon peas.

RICE
Basmati rice is the long-grain rice that gives an authentic Indian flavour to your cookery. Other long-grain rices include Patna and American, although if you use either of these as a substitute for Basmati, the flavour will not be as good.

ROSE WATER
This is used as a delicate flavouring for several Indian dishes. It is available from chemists' shops.

SAFFRON
The most expensive spice in the world, and no wonder: it is made from the orange stamens of a type of crocus flower, and it takes thousands of these to make just 25g/1oz of saffron. It is available in threads or ground form, and is used to colour and flavour rice, biryani dishes, sweets, puddings and cakes. Soak a few threads of saffron in hot water for about 15 minutes, then stir and add to the dish, together with the soaking water.

SESAME SEEDS
Usually white, but brown, red and black varieties are also available, sesame seeds can be toasted and sprinkled on sweet and savoury dishes, including breads, salads and spicy dishes.

TAMARIND
The dried fruit of the tamarind tree is known as 'Indian dates' because of its sticky appearance. The pods or pulp are soaked in hot water (see Cook's Tip, recipe 6) to yield tamarind water, which is sometimes used instead of vinegar or lemon juice to add sharpness to dishes.

TURMERIC
This is available in three forms: fresh, dried whole or, most commonly, ground. In its fresh form it looks like fresh root ginger. It is one of the most commonly used spices in Indian cookery, and is valued for its ability to add a bright golden colour to dishes in which it is used, and for its distinctive flavour. Use too much, however, and the flavour is overwhelming. It is one of the main components of curry powder, but is also used in some chutneys, pickles and relishes.

VARAK
Used to decorate both sweet and savoury dishes, this silver leaf is edible and makes a very unusual garnish. Never use aluminium foil as a substitute if you cannot obtain varak: provide another kind of simple garnish instead.

SOUPS, STARTERS & SNACKS

You can serve some of these snacks about 30 minutes before the main meal to sharpen the appetite, or incorporate them as part of the meal as a starter.

1 SPICED CHICKEN SOUP

Preparation time:
20 minutes

Cooking time:
about 1¼ hours

Serves 4-6

Calories:
480-320 per portion

YOU WILL NEED:
1.5 litres/2½ pints water
1 x 1.2 kg/2½ lb chicken, quartered
4 green King prawns, halved
salt and pepper
2 macadamia nuts, chopped
4 shallots, chopped
2 garlic cloves, chopped
2 teaspoons grated root ginger
pinch of turmeric
pinch of chilli powder
vegetable oil for shallow frying
1 tablespoon light soy sauce
about 75g/3 oz beansprouts
1 potato, peeled and cut into very thin rounds

Place the water in a pan and boil. Add the chicken, prawns and salt and pepper to taste. Cover and simmer for 40 minutes. Strain and reserve 1.2 litres/2 pints of the liquid. Shred the meat from the chicken and shell and chop the prawns.

Purée the macadamias, shallots, garlic and ginger in a liquidizer, add the turmeric and chilli powder and mix well.

Heat 2 tablespoons oil in a wok or frying pan, add the spice paste and fry for a few seconds. Stir in 300 ml/½ pint of the reserved liquid, the soy sauce, chicken and prawns. Simmer for 10 minutes. Add the remaining cooking liquid and simmer for a further 10 minutes. Add the beansprouts and cook for 3 minutes. Meanwhile, fry the potato slices in hot oil until crisp. Serve hot.

▌ COOK'S TIP

Macadamias are usually ready shelled and the kernels break into fragments. If 2 kemiri are specified in a recipe, this means the equivalent of 2 whole nuts.

2 FISH SOUP WITH COCONUT

Preparation time:
25 minutes

Cooking time:
about 15-20 minutes

Serves 4

Calories:
420 per portion

YOU WILL NEED:
550 g/1¼ lb monkfish or halibut fillet, skinned and cubed
salt
25 g/1 oz desiccated coconut
6 shallots
6 almonds, blanched
2-3 cloves garlic
1 x 2.5 cm/1 inch piece root ginger, peeled and sliced
2 stems lemon grass, trimmed and root discarded
2-3 teaspoons turmeric
3 tablespoons oil
1 recipe coconut cream and milk (see Cook's Tip)
1-2 fresh chillies, seeded and sliced
fresh coriander, to garnish

Sprinkle the fish with salt. Place the coconut in a wok and heat until golden and crisp. Remove and pound until oily. Purée the shallots, almonds, garlic, ginger and 6 cm/2½ inches from the root end of the lemon grass (reserve the remainder) in a blender. Add the turmeric.

Heat the oil and fry the puréed mixture for a few minutes. Add the coconut milk and bring to the boil, stirring constantly. Add the fish, chillies, remaining lemon grass and cook for 3-4 minutes. Stir in the pounded coconut and cook for 2-3 minutes. Remove the stems of lemon grass, stir in the coconut cream, transfer to a tureen and garnish with coriander.

▌ COOK'S TIP

For coconut cream and milk put 300 g/11 oz desiccated coconut and 750 ml/1¼ pints boiling water in a blender and work for 20 seconds. Pour into a bowl and cool to blood heat. Strain; this is the coconut milk. When the cream rises to the top of the milk skim off about 50 ml/2 fl oz and add to the soup just before serving.

3 MULLIGATAWNY SOUP

Preparation time:
30 minutes

Cooking time:
about 3 hours

Serves 6

Calories:
410 per portion

YOU WILL NEED:
450 g/1 lb shin of beef, cubed
1 kg /2 lb beef bones
about 2.25 litres/4 pints water
1 tablespoon coriander seeds
½ teaspoon black peppercorns
2 teaspoons cumin seeds
1 teaspoon turmeric
6 green cardamom pods
2-3 cloves
4 cloves garlic, crushed
salt
2 potatoes, peeled and diced
1 tablespoon oil
1 large onion, finely sliced
1 teaspoon garam masala
600 ml/1 pint coconut milk (see Cook's Tip, recipe 2)
juice of 1 lemon

Place the beef and bones and water in a pan. Add the spices, garlic, and salt to taste. Bring to the boil, skim, then cover and simmer for 2 hours. Cool slightly. Discard the bones and shred the meat finely.

Strain the soup and remove the spices. Return 1.75 litres/ 3 pints of the soup to the pan, add the potatoes and cook for 20 minutes. Stir in the reserved meat and set aside.

Heat the oil and fry the onion until golden. Add the garam masala, remove from the heat and stir in the coconut milk. Stir into the soup, add the lemon juice and reheat.

■ COOK'S TIP

This curried soup became popular in the days of the British Raj. It is delicious served with one of the Indian breads (recipes 188-92).

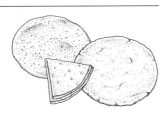

4 STUFFED PEPPERS

Preparation time:
20 minutes

Cooking time:
about 40 minutes

Serves 4

Calories:
470 per portion

YOU WILL NEED:
5 tablespoons oil
1 onion, finely chopped
2 teaspoons ground coriander
1 teaspoon ground cumin
½ teaspoon chilli powder
350 g/12 oz minced beef
3 tablespoons long-grain rice
salt
4 large green or red peppers, sliced lengthways, cored and seeded
1 x 400 g/14 oz can tomatoes

Heat 3 tablespoons of the oil in a pan. Add the onion and fry until golden. Add the spices and cook for 2 minutes. Add the minced beef and fry, stirring, until browned. Add the rice and salt to taste and cook for 2 minutes. Leave to cool, then fill the pepper shells with the mixture.

Heat the remaining oil in a pan just large enough to hold the peppers. Add the peppers, pour a little of the tomato juice into each pepper and the remaining juice and tomatoes into the pan, seasoning with salt to taste. Bring to simmering point, cover and cook for about 25 minutes, until the rice is tender.

■ COOK'S TIP

Stuffed Peppers make an excellent main course too, served with one or two breads (recipes 188-92) and a variety of salads, including Zalata (recipe 197), Raita (recipe 193) and Mixed Vegetable Raita (recipe 196).

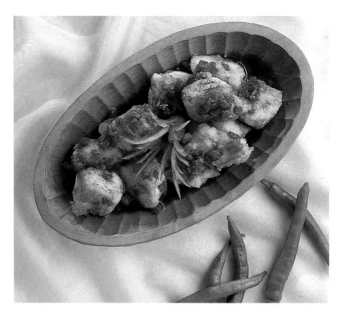

5 MEAT PUFFS

Preparation time:
15 minutes, plus 1
hour standing time

Cooking time:
about 10 minutes

Serves 4

Calories:
330 per portion

YOU WILL NEED:
3 tablespoons self-raising flour
3 eggs, beaten
5-6 tablespoons water
225 g/8 oz minced beef
1 bunch spring onions, trimmed and
    finely sliced
1 green chilli, finely chopped
1 teaspoon turmeric
salt
vegetable oil for frying

Sift the flour into a bowl, add the eggs and beat well to combine. Gradually add enough water to make a thick, creamy batter, beating well.

Stir in the minced beef, onions, chilli, turmeric and salt to taste; the mixture should be like stiff porridge. Leave in a warm place for 1 hour.

Heat about 1 cm/½ inch depth of oil in a frying pan. When really hot drop in spoonfuls of the meat mixture and fry on each side for 2 minutes. Drain well and keep warm while cooking the remainder, adding more oil as required. Serve hot.

6 AMOTIK

Preparation time:
15 minutes, plus 30
minutes soaking time

Cooking time:
20-25 minutes

Serves 4

Calories:
300 per portion

YOU WILL NEED:
50 g/2 oz tamarind (see Cook's Tip)
6 tablespoons hot water
4 tablespoons oil
675 g/1 ½ lb monkfish or other firm
    white fish, cubed
flour for dusting
1 onion, chopped
4 green chillies, finely chopped
2 garlic cloves, crushed
1 teaspoon ground cumin
½-1 teaspoon chilli powder
salt
1 tablespoon vinegar

Soak the tamarind in the water for 30 minutes, then strain, squeezing out as much water as possible. Discard the tamarind and reserve the water.

Heat the oil in a large pan. Lightly dust the fish with flour, add to the pan and fry quickly on both sides. Remove from the pan with a slotted spoon and set aside.

Add the onion to the pan and fry until soft and golden. Add the tamarind water, chillies, garlic, cumin, chilli powder and salt to taste and cook for 10 minutes. Add the fish and any juices and the vinegar. Simmer, uncovered, for about 5 minutes; be careful not to overcook.

▉ COOK'S TIP

To season a new iron frying
pan, heat 1 tablespoon oil
and plenty of salt together
until the salt begins to brown.
Wipe the inside of the pan
with absorbent paper.

▉ COOK'S TIP

Tamarind are pods from the
tamarind tree, used as a
souring agent. Sold as pods
or pulp, they must be soaked
in hot water, squeezed and
strained before use.

7   EGG MASALA

Preparation time:
20 minutes

Cooking time:
10-15 minutes

Serves 4

Calories:
300 per portion

YOU WILL NEED:
8 large eggs
5-6 sprigs fresh coriander leaves,
    chopped
1 medium onion, minced
4 medium tomatoes, chopped
1 tablespoon ground coriander
1 teaspoon chilli powder
salt
50 g/2 oz butter

Break the eggs into a bowl and beat well. Add all the remaining ingredients except the butter, and mix well.

Heat the butter in a frying pan and add the egg mixture. Stir-fry, breaking up any lumps of cooked egg, until the mixture resembles dry scrambled egg. Serve at once with triangles of toasted bread.

8   MIXED VEGETABLES

Preparation time:
25 minutes

Cooking time:
25-30 minutes

Serves 4

Calories:
150 per portion

YOU WILL NEED:
2-3 tablespoons oil
1 medium carrot, diced
1 medium onion, diced
1 medium potato, diced
1 small cauliflower, broken into florets
1 tablespoon ground coriander
1 tablespoon garam masala
1 teaspoon chilli powder
salt
5-6 sprigs fresh coriander leaves,
    coarsely chopped

Place the oil in a large pan over a low heat. Add all the ingredients and stir well. Cover and cook for about 25-30 minutes until the vegetables are tender.

Stir occasionally, making sure each time the lid is lifted that no water falls back into the vegetables. Serve hot or cold.

■ COOK'S TIP

Soak plates, cutlery and dishes encrusted with egg in cold water before washing up. Hot water glues the egg on to cutlery and crockery, making it tough to wash off.

■ COOK'S TIP

You can use a variety of root vegetables for this spicy, dry curry, according to taste and season. Cover it with cling film and it will keep for up to 5 days in the refrigerator.

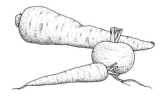

9 PRAWNS AND EGGS IN COCONUT SAUCE

Preparation time:
15 minutes

Cooking time:
20 minutes

Serves 4

Calories:
350 per portion

YOU WILL NEED:

550 g/1 ¼ lb peeled large prawns

5 macadamia nuts, chopped (see
   Cook's Tip, recipe 1)

3 red chillies, seeded and chopped

1 small onion, chopped

2 garlic cloves, chopped

½ teaspoon dried shrimp paste

2 teaspoons ground coriander

1 teaspoon grated root ginger

2 tablespoons oil

3 ripe tomatoes, chopped

salt

1 bay leaf

150 ml/¼ pint water

150 ml/¼ pint thick coconut milk

4 hard-boiled eggs, halved

75 g/3 oz mangetout, trimmed

Halve and de-vein the prawns. Put the macadamias, chillies, onion, garlic, shrimp paste, coriander and ginger in a liquidizer or food processor and purée.

Heat the oil in a wok or frying pan and fry the paste for 1 minute, stirring constantly. Add the prawns, tomatoes and salt to taste. Stir, cover and simmer for 2 minutes. Stir in the bay leaf and water. Increase the heat and boil, uncovered, 5 minutes.

Lower the heat, add the coconut milk and eggs and simmer for 8 minutes. Add the mangetout and simmer for 3 minutes. Transfer to a warmed serving dish and garnish as shown.

◼ COOK'S TIP

King prawns have a fine flavour but they are expensive. Instead you can use small peeled cooked prawns, in which case you will not have to de-vein them.

10 SWEET AND SOUR POTATO CURRY

Preparation time:
10-15 minutes

Cooking time:
25-30 minutes

Serves 4

Calories:
380 per portion

YOU WILL NEED:

50 ml/2 fl oz oil

1 teaspoon black mustard seeds

1 teaspoon cumin seeds

6 medium potatoes, cubed

2 teaspoons ground coriander

1 teaspoon turmeric

1 teaspoon chilli powder

2 teaspoons salt

4 teaspoons brown sugar

300 ml/½ pint water

1 x 75 g/3 oz can tomato purée

3 tablespoons vinegar

5-6 sprigs fresh coriander leaves,
   chopped, to garnish

Heat the oil in a pan, add the mustard and cumin seeds and fry them until they pop. Reduce the heat and carefully add the potatoes. Add all the remaining ingredients and stir well. Cover and cook over a low heat until the potatoes are tender and a large amount of thick sauce remains in the pan. Garnish with the chopped coriander and serve.

◼ COOK'S TIP

Black mustard seeds are used whole to flavour vegetable and pulse curries and other Asian dishes. Whole white mustard seeds are very good with cucumber – in salads, *pickles and chutneys, for example.*

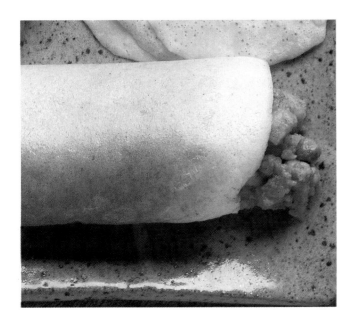

11 DOSAS

Preparation time:
10 minutes, plus
overnight soaking
time

Cooking time:
about 20 minutes

Makes 12-15

Calories:
120 per dosa

YOU WILL NEED:
225 g/8 oz urhad dal (dried pulses or
    lentils)
50 g/2 oz long-grain rice
600 ml/1 pint water
½ teaspoon bicarbonate of soda
1 teaspoon chilli powder
½ teaspoon salt
vegetable oil for shallow frying

Wash the dal and rice thoroughly, then put in a bowl with the
water and leave to soak overnight.

Place the dal, rice and water mixture in a blender or food
processor and work until smooth. Add the soda, chilli powder
and salt and stir well.

Pour in enough batter to cover the bottom of a cold
heavy-based pan. Put on the heat until the batter starts to set.
Pour about 1 tablespooon oil around the edge of the dosa,
then shake the pan to spread the oil. Fry the pancake for about
1 minute, until golden underneath. Remove from the pan and
roll up each dosa, enclosing a filling if liked. Repeat with the
remaining batter. Serve hot.

12 PAKORAS

Preparation time:
20 minutes, plus 2
hours standing time

Cooking time:
about 10 minutes

Serves 4

Calories:
180 per portion

YOU WILL NEED:
150 g/5 oz gram flour or bessan
½ teaspoon chilli powder
½ teaspoon salt
150 ml/¼ pint natural yogurt
1 teaspoon lemon juice
vegetable oil for deep frying
FOR THE FILLING
about 350 g/12 oz chopped mixed
    vegetables (cauliflower florets, cubed
    aubergine, sliced green peppers and
    sliced courgettes for example)

Sift the flour into a bowl, rubbing any lumps through the sieve
with the back of a spoon. Add the chilli powder and salt and
mix well. Gradually stir in the yogurt and lemon juice. Cover
and leave in a cool place for 2 hours until the batter is thick –
it should be much thicker than pancake batter.

Dip the vegetable pieces in the batter to coat, then deep
fry in hot oil until golden. Drain on absorbent kitchen paper.
Serve while warm and fresh.

■ COOK'S TIP

*You can serve Dosas as plain
pancakes, or filled – as here –
with a stuffing. Try filling
them with one of the spiced
and flavoured rices (recipes
173-85).*

■ COOK'S TIP

*This batter may be cooked
plain without the vegetables
if liked. Pakoras will keep in
an airtight container for a
few days. Reheat under the
grill before serving.*

13   GRILLED LIVER

Preparation time:
10 minutes, plus 30 minutes marinating time

Cooking time:
about 20 minutes

Serves 4

Calories:
460 per portion

YOU WILL NEED:
50 ml/2 fl oz oil
1 tablespoon ground cumin
1 teaspoon garlic powder
1 teaspoon chilli powder
2 teaspoons salt
1 tablespoon tomato purée
1 tablespoon brown sugar
1 tablespoon lemon juice
4 portions lamb's liver, about
175 g/6 oz each, each piece cut in 2
FOR THE GARNISH
1 small lettuce, shredded
1 lime, sliced

Place all the ingredients except the liver in a large bowl and mix thoroughly. Spread the mixture over the liver until every piece is well coated. Cover and leave to marinate for 30 minutes.

Before cooking, toss the liver well in the mixture. Place the liver on the rack in a grill pan and cook under a moderate grill for 10 minutes on each side. Serve immediately on a bed of shredded lettuce, garnished with lime slices.

14   CHICKEN TIKKA

Preparation time:
15 minutes, plus overnight marinating time

Cooking time:
5-6 minutes

Serves 4

Calories:
200 per portion

YOU WILL NEED:
675 g/1 ½ lb chicken breasts
FOR THE MARINADE
150 ml/¼ pint natural yogurt
1 tablespoon grated root ginger
2 garlic cloves, crushed
1 teaspoon chilli powder
1 tablespoon ground coriander
½ teaspoon salt
juice of 1 lemon
2 tablespoons oil
FOR THE GARNISH
1 onion, sliced
2 tomatoes, quartered
4 lemon twists

Skin, bone and cube the chicken breasts. Mix all the marinade ingredients together in a bowl. Add the chicken cubes, stir well and leave in the refrigerator overnight.

Thread the chicken on to 4 skewers and cook under a hot grill for 5-6 minutes, turning frequently.

Remove the chicken from the skewers and arrange on individual serving plates. Garnish with onion, tomato and lemon to serve.

■ COOK'S TIP

Liver should look smooth and glossy when you buy it. Before cooking, remove all the tubes, outside membrane and tough parts using a pointed knife.

■ COOK'S TIP

To make lemon twists, thinly slice a lemon and cut a slit in to the centre of each slice. Twist the slices from the cuts.

15 STEAMED LENTIL CAKES

Preparation time:
15 minutes, plus
overnight soaking
time

Cooking time:
1 hour

Oven temperature:
190C, 375F, gas 5

Makes 6-8

Calories:
210-160 per portion

YOU WILL NEED:
350 g/12 oz red lentils
1.75 litres/3 pints cold water
1 teaspoon ground cumin
1 teaspoon chilli powder
1 teaspoon salt
½ teaspoon black peppercorns, crushed
25 g/1 oz fresh coriander leaves,
*   chopped*
juice of 1 lemon
225 g/8 oz natural yogurt

Wash the lentils. Drain, place in a bowl and add the cold water. Let soak overnight. Drain off the water and grind the lentils to a fine paste in a food processor. Using muslin or a strong tea towel, squeeze the excess water from the lentils.

Transfer the lentil paste to a bowl and add the cumin, chilli powder, salt, pepper and coriander leaves. Shape into 6-8 cakes, 5 cm/2 inches in diameter and 1 cm/½ inch thick. Pat them dry with absorbent kitchen paper.

Place the cakes in the top of a steamer, cover and steam for 1 hour. Alternatively, place the cakes in a shallow dish, stand it in a roasting tin filled with enough hot water to come halfway up the sides of the dish. Cover the dish and tin with cooking foil, then bake for 1 hour. Remove and allow to cool.

Mix the lemon juice with the yogurt. Place the lentil cakes in a shallow dish and cover with the yogurt mixture. Refrigerate for at least 2 hours before serving.

■ COOK'S TIP

Just like any other pulses, red lentils can be sprouted by placing them in a jar with a piece of gauze stretched over the neck of it. Cover the pulses with clean water, then *drain them and repeat this process at least twice daily until they sprout in a few days.*

16 EKURI

Preparation time:
10 minutes

Cooking time:
5-10 minutes

Serves 4

Calories:
300 per portion

YOU WILL NEED:
50 g/2 oz butter
1 onion, finely chopped
2 green chillies, finely chopped
8 eggs, lightly beaten with 2 tablespoons
*   water*
1 tablespoon finely chopped fresh
*   coriander leaves*
salt

Heat the butter in a pan, add the onion and fry until deep golden. Add the chillies and fry for 30 seconds, then add the eggs, coriander and salt to taste. Cook, stirring constantly, until the eggs are lightly scrambled and set. Serve hot.

■ COOK'S TIP

Hot, fresh green chillies should be used for this recipe, but use with care. For a less pungent result slit the chillies, discard the seeds and rinse under a tap.

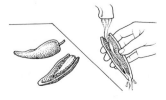

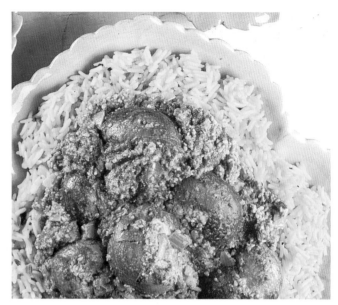

17 NIMKI

Preparation time:
15 minutes

Cooking time:
10 minutes

Serves 4-6

Calories:
380-260 per portion

YOU WILL NEED:
225 g/8 oz plain flour
1 teaspoon salt
1 teaspoon caster sugar
1 teaspoon onion seeds
15 g/½ oz butter or ghee
1 ripe banana, peeled and mashed
600 ml/1 pint oil for deep frying

Sift the flour, salt and sugar into a bowl and add the onion seeds. Rub in the butter or ghee, add the banana and enough water to make a soft, smooth dough. Roll out very thinly to about 3 mm/⅛ inch thickness. Cut the dough diagonally into strips both ways to make small diamond shapes, and prick with a fork.

Heat the oil in a pan and fry the shapes until golden brown and crisp. Drain on absorbent kitchen paper and allow to cool.

18 SESAME KIDNEYS

Preparation time:
20 minutes

Cooking time:
30-35 minutes

Serves 4

Calories:
440 per portion

YOU WILL NEED:
100 g/4 oz butter
1 large onion, minced
100 g/4 oz sesame seeds, finely ground
1 x 225 g/8 oz can tomatoes, chopped
  with the juice
150 ml/¼ pint water
1 teaspoon garam masala
1 tablespoon lemon juice
1 tablespoon sugar
salt
350 g/12 oz lamb's kidneys, halved and
  cored

Melt the butter in a pan and fry the onion until soft. Add the sesame seeds and fry for 1-2 minutes. Stir in the tomatoes, water, garam masala, lemon juice, sugar and salt, and cook for 10 minutes.

Add the kidneys to the sauce and stir well. Cover and cook over a low heat for about 20 minutes until tender. Be sure not to overcook the kidneys as they will toughen if cooked longer than necessary. Serve hot.

■ COOK'S TIP

Nimki can be sweet or savoury, flavoured with a variety of vegetables, fruit or essences. To make savoury Nimki, add either chilli powder or black pepper to the ingredients in the recipe above, and omit the banana and sugar.

■ COOK'S TIP

Prepare kidneys by pulling off the fine membrane that covers them, cutting them in half lengthwise and snipping out the core with a sharp pair of scissors.

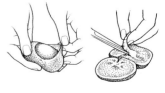

19 SAMOSAS

Preparation time:
30 minutes

Cooking time:
about 20 minutes

Makes about 24

Calories:
200 per samosa

YOU WILL NEED:
225 g/8 oz plain flour
3 tablespoons ghee
½ teaspoon salt
about 250 ml/8 fl oz milk, soured with a
*   little lemon juice*
vegetable oil for deep frying
FOR THE FILLING
1 recipe Vegetable Kheema (see recipe
*   70)*

Sift the flour into a bowl, rub in the ghee, then add the salt. Gradually stir in the milk to form a stiff dough. Chill until required.

Break the dough into pieces, about 2.5 cm/1 inch in diameter. Roll into very thin circles, then cut each circle in half. Spoon a little of the filling into the centre of each semi-circle, then fold in half to make a triangular cone shape, enclosing the filling. Moisten the edges of the dough with soured milk and seal well.

Heat the oil and deep fry the samosas, a few at a time, for about 1 minute until the pastry is golden. Drain the Samosas well and serve them warm.

20 SPICED FRIED PRAWNS

Preparation time:
15 minutes, plus 30 minutes marinating time

Cooking time:
about 10 minutes

Serves 4

Calories:
300 per portion

YOU WILL NEED:
450 g/1 lb cooked prawns
2 tablespoons tamarind water
pinch of turmeric
1 teaspoon grated root ginger
2 shallots or ½ onion, sliced
2 garlic cloves, crushed
1 tablespoon light soy sauce
150 ml/¼ pint oil
FOR THE BATTER
75 g/3 oz rice flour or plain flour
4 tablespoons water
salt and pepper
1 small egg, beaten

Discard the heads and shells from the prawns, but leave on the tails. De-vein them. Place in a bowl with the tamarind water, turmeric, ginger, shallots, garlic and soy sauce. Stir well and leave to marinate for 30 minutes.

Meanwhile, make the batter. Place the flour in a bowl and gradually add the water. Add salt and pepper to taste, then gradually beat in the egg.

Drain the marinade from the prawns and shallots. Dip the prawns and shallots in the batter. Heat the oil in a frying pan or wok and add the prawns and shallots, one at a time, until the bottom is covered. Fry until golden brown and crisp, then turn over and fry the underside. Serve hot or cold.

■ COOK'S TIP

To make ghee, place 225 g/ 8 oz unsalted butter in a pan over a low heat. Bring almost to simmering point and cook gently for 20-30 minutes until it begins to change colour.

Strain into a screw-topped jar through several thicknesses of muslin. Though refrigeration is not necessary, keep the ghee in a cool place.

■ COOK'S TIP

This dish should really be made with freshly cooked prawns, but is still delicious with pre-cooked prawns from the fishmonger. Serve it with Basmati rice.

FISH & SEAFOOD DISHES

Curries and milder dishes, as well as recipes for fried, grilled, steamed and baked fish and shellfish are all to be found in this chapter.

21 GRILLED SPICED FISH

Preparation time:
10 minutes, plus 2 hours marinating time

Cooking time:
6-8 minutes

Serves 4

Calories:
220 per portion

YOU WILL NEED:
2 large or 4 small plaice, cleaned
150 g/5 oz natural yogurt
2 garlic cloves, crushed
1 teaspoon ground coriander seeds
½ teaspoon chilli powder
1 teaspoon garam masala
1 tablespoon vinegar
1 tablespoon oil
salt

Slash the fish on both sides and place in separate shallow dishes. Mix the remaining ingredients together adding salt to taste, and divide between the fish. Spoon it all over one side and leave for 1 hour, then turn and spoon over the juice that has collected in the dish. Leave to marinate for another hour.

Cook under a moderate grill for 3-4 minutes. Turn and baste with any juices collected in the grill pan, then cook for a further 3-4 minutes and serve at once.

22 SPINACH WITH PRAWNS

Preparation time:
10 minutes

Cooking time:
20 minutes

Serves 4

Calories:
270 per portion

YOU WILL NEED:
50 g/2 oz ghee
1 large onion, sliced
2 garlic cloves, sliced
1 tablespoon tomato purée
½ teaspoon garam masala
1 ½ teaspoons ground coriander
½ teaspoon turmeric
½ teaspoon chilli powder
½ teaspoon ground ginger
1 teaspoon salt
450 g/1 lb frozen whole leaf spinach
450 g/1 lb peeled prawns

Melt the ghee in a large saucepan, add the onion and garlic and fry gently for 4-5 minutes until soft. Stir in the tomato purée and fry, stirring constantly, for 1 minute. Add the spices and salt and fry for a further 5 minutes, stirring constantly.

Add the frozen spinach and break up with a wooden spoon. Cook until the spinach has thoroughly defrosted, about 3-4 minutes, stirring frequently. Add the prawns and cook for a further 5 minutes, turning gently to coat with the spinach. Serve at once.

■ COOK'S TIP

For garam masala place 2 tablespoons black peppercorns, 1 tablespoon black cumin seeds, 1 small cinnamon stick, 1 teaspoon cloves, ¼ nutmeg,

2 teaspoons cardamom seeds and 2 tablespoons coriander seeds in a coffee grinder or pestle and mortar and grind to a powder. Store in a jar.

■ COOK'S TIP

Ghee is better than butter for cooking as it can be heated to a higher temperature without burning. However, if you prefer, you can substitute 4 tablespoons oil in this recipe.

23   HADDOCK IN CHILLI SAUCE

Preparation time:
5 minutes

Cooking time:
15-20 minutes

Serves 4

Calories:
350 per portion

YOU WILL NEED:
4 tablespoons oil
2 large onions, sliced
3 cloves garlic, crushed
750 g/1 ½ lb haddock fillets, cut into
   chunks
2 tablespoons plain flour
1 teaspoon turmeric
4 green chillies, thinly sliced
2 tablespoons lemon juice
175 ml/6 fl oz thick coconut milk (see
   Cook's Tip, recipe 2)
salt
chilli flowers to garnish (see Cook's Tip)

Heat the oil in a wok, add the onions and fry until soft and golden. Add the garlic and cook for 30 seconds. Remove from the pan with a slotted spoon and set aside.

Toss the fish in the flour, add to the pan and brown quickly on all sides. Drain on kitchen paper.

Return the onions and garlic to the wok, stir in the turmeric and chillies; cook for 1 minute. Stir in the lemon juice, coconut milk and salt to taste; simmer, uncovered, for 10 minutes, stirring until the sauce has thickened.

Return the fish to the wok and heat for 2-3 minutes. Spoon into a warmed serving dish and serve garnished with chilli flowers.

24   FISH TANDOORI

Preparation time:
30 minutes, plus 4-5
hours marinating time

Cooking time:
20-25 minutes

Oven temperature:
180C, 350F, gas 4

Serves 4

Calories:
260 per portion

YOU WILL NEED:
4 halibut steaks, about 175 g/6 oz each
50 g/2 oz natural yogurt
2 tablespoons oil
2 tablespoons paprika
1 tablespoon ground cumin
1 teaspoon ground fennel seeds
1 teaspoon chilli powder
salt
FOR THE GARNISH
1 small lettuce, shredded
1 fennel bulb, sliced

Wash and pat the fish dry using absorbent kitchen paper.

Combine all the remaining ingredients in a large bowl and mix well. Place the fish in the bowl and rub well with the tandoori mixture. Cover and leave to marinate for 4-5 hours.

Transfer the marinated fish to a shallow ovenproof baking dish and bake uncovered for 20-25 minutes. Arrange the lettuce on a warmed serving dish. Lift the fish on to the lettuce and spoon over the juices. Garnish with the fennel and serve at once.

■ COOK'S TIP

To make chilli flowers, shred the chilli lengthways, leaving 1 cm/½ inch attached at the stem end. Place in iced water for about 1 hour to open.

■ COOK'S TIP

Fennel is a versatile plant – its leaves be used as a garnish, and the bulbous part is good in salads with vinaigrette dressing, or baked with a cheese or tomato sauce.

25 FISH MOLEE

Preparation time:
10 minutes

Cooking time:
20-25 minutes

Serves 4

Calories:
400 per portion

YOU WILL NEED:
675 g/1½ lb cod fillet, skinned and cut
    into 4 pieces
2 tablespoons plain flour
4 tablespoons oil
2 onions, sliced
2 garlic cloves, crushed
1 teaspoon turmeric
4 green chillies, finely chopped
2 tablespoons lemon juice
175 ml/6 fl oz thick coconut milk (see
    Cook's Tip, recipe 2)
salt

Coat the fish with the flour. Heat the oil in a frying pan, add the fish and fry quickly on both sides. Remove with a slotted spoon and set aside.

Add the onion and garlic to the pan and fry until soft and golden. Add the turmeric, chillies, lemon juice, coconut milk and salt to taste. Simmer, uncovered for 10 minutes or until thickened.

Add the fish and any juices, spoon over the sauce and cook gently for 2-3 minutes, until tender.

26 PRAWN CHILLI FRY

Preparation time:
5 minutes

Cooking time:
10 minutes

Serves 4

Calories:
180 per portion

YOU WILL NEED:
3 tablespoons oil
3 onions, sliced
2 green chillies, seeded and chopped
1 x 2.5 cm/1 inch piece root ginger,
    chopped
½ teaspoon chilli powder
½ teaspoon turmeric
salt
225 g/8 oz frozen prawns

Heat the oil in a pan, add the onions and fry until soft and golden. Add the chillies, ginger, chilli powder, turmeric and salt to taste and fry for 2 minutes.

Add the prawns and cook, uncovered, for about 3 minutes or until all the moisture has evaporated.

▨ COOK'S TIP

When shallow-frying fish fillets, place them in the pan boned side down first to prevent them breaking up.

▨ COOK'S TIP

Turmeric can sometimes be bought fresh – it looks like fresh root ginger – but is normally obtained in ground form. Its bright golden colouring enhances dishes
such as this, but be warned: it also stains clothing and work surfaces!

27   VINEGAR FISH

Preparation time:
10 minutes

Cooking time:
12-15 minutes

Serves 4

Calories:
260 per portion

YOU WILL NEED:
1 teaspoon turmeric
1 teaspoon salt
450 g/1 lb haddock or cod steaks
3 tablespoons oil
2 onions, sliced
2-3 green chillies, thinly sliced
2 garlic cloves
1 x 2.5 cm/1 inch piece root ginger, cut
into strips
2 tablespoons white wine vinegar
4 tablespoons water
fresh coriander leaves, to garnish

Mix the turmeric and salt together on a plate. Coat the fish in the mixture. Heat the oil in a frying pan, add the fish and fry gently on both sides for 1-2 minutes. Lift out the fish and set aside.

Add the onions, chillies, garlic and ginger to the pan and fry, stirring, until golden. Stir in the vinegar and water. Put in the fish, cover and cook gently for 5-6 minutes or until cooked through.

Transfer to a warmed serving dish and garnish with the coriander to serve.

28   FISH CURRY

Preparation time:
15 minutes

Cooking time:
about 20 minutes

Serves 4-6

Calories:
220-150 per portion

YOU WILL NEED:
40 g /1 ½ oz ghee or 3 tablespoons oil
2 onions, chopped
25g/1 oz root ginger, peeled and crushed
4-5 garlic cloves, crushed
½ teaspoon turmeric
about 1 teaspoon chilli powder
1 teaspoon ground cumin
1 teaspoon ground coriander
1 teaspoon garam masala
450 g/1 lb white fish fillets, cut into
2.5 cm/1 inch pieces
1 x 400 g/14 oz can tomatoes
1 teaspoon salt
1 green chilli, halved and seeded
FOR THE GARNISH
1 green pepper, seeded and finely
chopped
finely chopped fresh coriander leaves

Heat the ghee or oil in a large saucepan and fry the onion. Add the ginger, garlic, turmeric, chilli powder, cumin, ground coriander and garam masala. Fry for 15 seconds, then add the fish pieces and stir gently.

Add the tomatoes, salt and chilli. Cover and simmer gently for 5-10 minutes or until the fish is tender. Remove from the heat and add the green pepper and chopped coriander. Remove the chilli if preferred, and serve at once.

■ COOK'S TIP

This is a recipe from the west coast of India. Here sourness is introduced with vinegar instead of the usual way with tamarind. Serve with lentils, chapati and natural yogurt.

■ COOK'S TIP

Cod, hake, halibut, coley, haddock, plaice or whiting are all suitable for this recipe. Use frozen fish, if liked, adding it towards the end of the cooking time.

29 GOAN MACKEREL CURRY

Preparation time:
about 20 minutes,
plus about
30 minutes
soaking time

Cooking time:
30-40 minutes

Serves 4-6

Calories:
380-260 per portion

YOU WILL NEED:
15 g/½ oz tamarind pods
2 tablespoons oil
1 small onion, chopped
about 1 teaspoon chilli powder
½ teaspoon ground cumin
2 teaspoons ground coriander
100 g/4 oz desiccated coconut
½ teaspoon turmeric
½ of 1 x 225 g/8 oz can tomatoes,
    roughly chopped
5-6 curry leaves
1-2 green chillies, very finely chopped
salt
7 fl oz/ ⅓ pint water
450 g/1 lb mackerel, cleaned and cut
    into 2.5 cm/1 inch pieces

Soak the tamarind pods in half a teacup of hot water for 10-15 minutes and extract the pulp. Repeat this process to extract any remaining pulp.

Heat the oil in a large saucepan and fry the onion until lightly browned. Add the chilli powder, cumin, coriander, coconut and turmeric. Fry for 30 seconds.

Stir in the tomatoes, tamarind pulp, curry leaves, chilli and salt. Add the water. Carefully stir in the mackerel, cover and simmer gently for 20-30 minutes until the fish is tender. Serve at once.

30 PRAWN AND EGG SAMBAL

Preparation time:
10 minutes, plus 1
hour chilling time

Serves 4

Calories:
240 per portion

YOU WILL NEED:
450 g/1 lb peeled prawns
4 hard-boiled eggs, shelled and
    quartered
300 ml/½ pint coconut milk
1 small onion, minced
1 garlic clove, crushed
1 green chilli, seeded and chopped
juice of ½ lemon
pinch of chilli powder
½ teaspoon salt
FOR THE GARNISH
50 g/2 oz cooked green peas
finely chopped fresh coriander leaves

Arrange the prawns and eggs in a shallow serving dish, then chill in the refrigerator for about 1 hour.

Place the coconut milk, onion, garlic, chilli, lemon juice, chilli powder and salt in a food processor or liquidizer and purée until smooth. Pour over the prawn and egg mixture. Garnish with the peas and coriander and chill before serving.

■ COOK'S TIP

Unfilleted mackerel is used in this recipe for its flavour and appearance, but filleted mackerel may be used instead if you prefer.

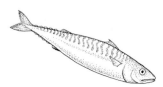

■ COOK'S TIP

Fresh prawns are usually sold boiled in the shell, and all you have to do is pull off the heads and tails and shell them. Boil uncooked prawns for about 10 minutes in *salted water and shell them when cool.*

31 PINEAPPLE PRAWN CURRY

Preparation time:
15 minutes

Cooking time:
15 minutes

Serves 4

Calories:
450 per portion

YOU WILL NEED:
2 garlic cloves
1 small onion, quartered
2 green chillies, chopped
50 g/2 oz butter
1 bunch spring onions, chopped
450 g/1 lb raw peeled prawns
1 large green pepper, cored, seeded and
   coarsely chopped
150 ml/¼ pint double cream
salt
1 small pineapple, cut into chunks

Put the garlic, onion and green chillies in a liquidizer or food processor and work to a paste.

Melt the butter in a large frying pan, add the spring onions, prawns and green pepper and cook, stirring constantly until the prawns turn pink. Add the prepared paste and fry, stirring, for 2 minutes.

Add the cream, a spoonful at a time, and when it has all been in corporated, season with salt to taste. Stir in the pineapple. Cover and simmer for 5 minutes, then serve at once.

32 PICKLED HADDOCK STEAKS

Preparation time:
15 minutes, plus 12
hours chilling time

Cooking time:
about 20 minutes

Serves 4

Calories:
340 per portion

YOU WILL NEED:
4 tablespoons oil
4 x 225 g/8 oz haddock steaks
2 onions, chopped
1 garlic clove, peeled
1 x 2.5 cm/1 inch piece root ginger,
   peeled
1 tablespoon coriander seeds
4 green chillies, seeded
5 tablespoons wine vinegar
½ teaspoon turmeric
4 curry leaves
salt

Heat the oil in a large frying pan, add the fish and fry on both sides until browned. Remove with a slotted spoon and set aside. Add the onions to the pan and fry until soft.

Put the garlic, ginger, coriander seeds, chillies and 1 tablespoon vinegar into a liquidizer or food processor and work to a paste. Add to the pan with the turmeric, curry leaves and salt to taste and fry for 3-4 minutes.

Add the remaining vinegar, bring to simmering point, stir well and add the fish. Cook, uncovered, for 3-4 minutes, until tender.

Place the fish in a dish, pour over all the juices and leave to cool. Cover and keep in the refrigerator for at least 12 hours. Serve cold.

■ COOK'S TIP

To prepare fresh pineapple, cut off the top, slice the flesh and peel it, and then cut out the hard, woody core. Canned pineapple chunks are too sweet to use here.

■ COOK'S TIP

This is excellent served with Naan bread (recipe 192) and a rice dish, such as Tomato Rice (recipe 178) or Tahiri (recipe 180).

33 MADRAS DRY PRAWN CURRY

Preparation time:
5 minutes

Cooking time:
about 10 minutes

Serves 4

Calories:
230 per portion

YOU WILL NEED:
50 g/2 oz ghee
1 small onion, sliced
2 garlic cloves, sliced
1 teaspoon ground coriander
½ teaspoon turmeric
pinch of ground ginger
½ teaspoon ground cumin
½ teaspoon salt
450 g/1 lb peeled prawns
1 tablespoon vinegar
pinch of chilli powder, to garnish

Melt the ghee in a large saucepan, add the onion and garlic and fry gently for 4-5 minutes until soft. Add the coriander, turmeric, ginger, cumin and salt and fry for a further 3 minutes, stirring constantly.

Reduce the heat, then add the prawns and toss lightly for 1 minute until coated with the spices. Stir in the vinegar, increase the heat and cook for 30 seconds. Sprinkle with the chilli powder and serve immediately.

34 PRAWNS WITH TAMARIND

Preparation time:
10 minutes, plus
1 hour for the
tamarind paste

Cooking time:
about 10 minutes

Serves 4

Calories:
300 per portion

YOU WILL NEED:
225 g/8 oz tamarind
100 ml/4 fl oz water
1 small red pepper, cored, seeded and
    chopped
25 g/1 oz small onions, chopped
2 garlic cloves, chopped
1 red chilli, seeded and chopped
1 tablespoon ground lemon grass
6 tablespoons oil
4 teaspoons caster sugar
2 teaspoons lime juice
salt
450 g/1 lb unpeeled Mediterranean
    prawns, heads left on and de-veined
    through the shell

To make the tamarind paste, place the tamarind and water in a small pan and bring to the boil. Cover and simmer for 10 minutes. Remove from the heat and leave to stand, covered, for 1 hour. Mash, then sieve into a bowl. Reserve 3 tablespoons and use the remainder for another dish.

Place the red pepper, onions, garlic, chilli and lemon grass in a liquidizer or food processor and blend. Heat the oil, add the pepper mixture and stir-fry for 5 minutes. Gradually blend in the tamarind paste, sugar, lime juice and salt to taste. Add the prawns and stir-fry for 5 minutes or until the prawns are just firm to the touch. Serve at once.

■ COOK'S TIP

The lack of liquid in dry curries such as this tends to concentrate the spiciness of the dish, so serve a suitable drink such as iced water, chilled lager or a light beer.

■ COOK'S TIP

The tamarind paste can be stored in the refrigerator for use in other dishes for up to 2 weeks.

35   DRY FRIED HERRING

Preparation time:
about 20 minutes

Cooking time:
30 minutes

Serves 4

Calories:
260 per portion

YOU WILL NEED:
about 1 teaspoon chilli powder
1½ teaspoons turmeric
1 teaspoon ground ginger
1 teaspoon garlic powder or paste
salt and pepper
450 g/1 lb herring fillets, cut into 5 cm/
*   2 inch pieces*
oil for frying
1 lemon, sliced, to garnish

Mix together the chilli powder, turmeric, ginger, garlic and salt and pepper to taste. Rub this mixture into the fish and set aside to marinate for 10-15 minutes.

Heat a little oil and fry the fish in two batches until golden brown. Remove and drain the fish. Serve hot, garnished with lemon slices.

36   MACHI MUSSALAM

Preparation time:
15 minutes, plus
marinating time

Cooking time:
15 minutes

Serves 4

Calories:
360 per portion

YOU WILL NEED:
1 kg/2 lb cod steaks
1 teaspoon salt
150 g/5 oz natural yogurt
4 tablespoons oil
2 onions, finely sliced
1 x 2.5 cm/1 inch piece root ginger,
*   finely sliced*
4 green chillies, seeded
2 garlic cloves
1 teaspoon fenugreek seeds
coriander leaves, to garnish (optional)

Sprinkle the fish with the salt and marinate it in the yogurt for about 1 hour, turning once or twice.

Heat 1 tablespoon of the oil in a pan, add one of the onions and fry until crisp. Place this, together with the remaining onion, the ginger, chillies and garlic in a food processor or liquidizer and work to a smooth paste.

Heat the remaining oil in a large frying pan with a lid. Fry the fenugreek seeds for 30 seconds, then add the prepared paste and fry until it starts to brown. Add the fish and yogurt. Stir carefully and spoon the mixture over the fish. Cover and simmer for 5-10 minutes until cooked through; if too dry, add 2 tablespoons water; if too liquid, uncover.

Transfer to a warmed serving dish and garnish with coriander, if using.

■ COOK'S TIP

The herring is a bony, delicately flavoured fish and because of this it is generally fried rather than made into a curry. Cut the herring into pieces with or without the roe.

■ COOK'S TIP

Machi Mussalam is a dish from the Bombay area. Either steaks or fillets of cod can be used, but it is important that the fish should remain firm during cooking.

37 PRAWN CURRY

Preparation time:
10 minutes

Cooking time:
25 minutes

Serves 4

Calories:
280 per portion

YOU WILL NEED:
2 tablespoons oil
1 large onion, chopped
175 g/6 oz tomatoes, peeled and
chopped
½ teaspoon turmeric
1 teaspoon mustard seeds
½ teaspoon chilli powder
2 tablespoons natural yogurt
5 garlic cloves, crushed
½ teaspoon fenugreek
salt
300 ml/½ pint water
450 g/1 lb peeled prawns
juice of ½ lemon
chopped fresh coriander, to garnish

Heat the oil in a large frying pan, add the onion and fry gently until golden brown. Add all the remaining ingredients except the prawns and lemon juice. Cook for 10 minutes, stirring occasionally. Add the prawns and lemon juice and cook for a further 10 minutes. Serve immediately, garnished with coriander.

38 TANDOORI SOLE

Preparation time:
10 minutes, plus
marinating time

Cooking time:
15 minutes

Oven temperature:
180C, 350F, gas 4

Serves 2

Calories:
300 per portion

YOU WILL NEED:
½ teaspoon chilli powder
½ teaspoon turmeric
½ teaspoon ground coriander
½ teaspoon ground cumin
1 teaspoon ground ginger
½ teaspoon garam masala
salt and pepper
275 g/10 oz natural yogurt
2 garlic cloves, crushed
2 drops red food colouring
2 lemon sole, skinned and filleted (see
Cook's Tip)

Mix all the spices together, adding salt and pepper to taste. Add to the yogurt with the garlic and food colouring and stir well. Mix with the fish and leave to marinate for 1 hour.

Pour boiling water into a roasting pan to come halfway up the sides. Put a grill rack in the pan and place the marinated fish on the rack. Pour any remaining marinade over the fish. Cook for 15 minutes. Garnish as shown if liked. Serve at once.

▪ COOK'S TIP

Serve this with Plain Boiled
Rice (recipe 175), and a
selection of accompaniments
such as chutney (recipes 201-
11), Raita (recipe 193) and
crushed pineapple.

▪ COOK'S TIP

To skin fish, place the fish
skin down on a board and
hold the tail end. With a
sharp knife, cut between the
skin and flesh at an acute
angle, working from the tail.

39 PRAWN AND EGG CURRY

Preparation time:
10 minutes

Cooking time:
35 minutes

Serves 4

Calories:
370 per portion

YOU WILL NEED:
4 tablespoons oil
1 large onion, chopped
1 garlic clove, chopped
1 x 2.5 cm/1 inch piece root ginger,
   chopped
1 tablespoon ground coriander seeds
2 teaspoons ground cumin seeds
1 teaspoon chilli powder
1 tablespoon tomato purée
300 ml/½ pint water
salt
6 hard-boiled eggs, shelled and halved
225 g/8 oz frozen prawns
25 g/1 oz creamed coconut

Heat the oil in a saucepan, add the onion and fry until golden. Add the garlic and ginger and fry for 1 minute. Add the coriander, cumin and chilli powder and fry gently for 2 minutes, stirring occasionally; if the mixture becomes too dry, add 1 tablespoon water. Add the tomato purée, mix well, then add the water and salt to taste. Cover and simmer for 10 minutes.

Add the eggs, spooning some mixture over them. Cover and cook for 15 minutes, stirring occasionally. Stir in the prawns. When the curry starts to simmer again, stir in the creamed coconut. Bring to simmering point once more, then serve immediately.

40 SPICED PRAWNS IN COCONUT

Preparation time:
5 minutes

Cooking time:
15 minutes

Serves 4

Calories:
280 per portion

YOU WILL NEED:
4 tablespoons oil
1 large onion, sliced
4 garlic cloves, sliced
2 teaspoons ground coriander
1 teaspoon turmeric
1 teaspoon chilli powder
½ tespoon ground ginger
½ teaspoon salt
pepper to taste
2 tablespoons vinegar
200 ml/½ pint coconut milk (see Cook's
   Tip, recipe 2)
2 tablespoons tomato purée
450 g/1 lb peeled prawns

Heat the oil in a wok or deep frying pan, add the onion and garlic and fry gently until soft and golden.

Mix the spices together in a bowl, add the salt and pepper, stir in the vinegar and mix to a paste. Add to the wok and fry for 3 minutes, stirring constantly.

Stir in the coconut milk and tomato purée and simmer for 5 minutes. Stir in the prawns and heat through for 2-3 minutes, until well coated with sauce. Serve at once garnished as shown if liked.

■ COOK'S TIP

To ensure eggs don't crack or become misshapen when boiling, prick them at the blunt end with an egg pricker or small needle to allow the air inside to escape.

■ COOK'S TIP

To make decorative lemon slices as shown, drag a canelle knife down the lemon at evenly spaced intervals before slicing. Decorate cucumber in a similar way.

41 BOMBAY FISH CURRY

Preparation time:
10 minutes

Cooking time:
15-20 minutes

Serves 4

Calories:
160 per portion

YOU WILL NEED:
2 tablespoons oil
2 tablespoons finely chopped onion
2 garlic cloves, crushed
1 tablespoon finely chopped root ginger
½ teaspoon chilli powder
4 green chillies, seeded and finely
    chopped
300 ml/½ pint thin coconut milk
salt
4 fish cutlets (halibut or cod for
    example)

Heat the oil in a saucepan, add the onion, garlic, ginger and chilli powder and fry until the onion is soft. Add the chillies, coconut milk and salt to taste and simmer until thickened. Add the fish, spooning the sauce over, and cook, uncovered, for about 5 minutes or until tender. Serve hot.

42 KING PRAWNS IN SPICY DRESSING

Preparation time:
10 minutes

Cooking time:
10 minutes

Serves 4

Calories:
150 per portion

YOU WILL NEED:
50 g/2 oz ghee
1 large onion, chopped
2 garlic cloves, chopped
2 green chillies, seeded and chopped
1 teaspoon turmeric
½ teaspoon ground ginger
½ teaspoon ground cumin
½ teaspoon chilli powder
2 tablespoons coconut milk
12 King prawns

Melt the ghee in a heavy-based frying pan, add the onion and garlic and fry gently for 4-5 minutes until soft. Add the chillies, turmeric, ginger, cumin and chilli powder and fry for a further 3 minutes, stirring constantly. Add the coconut milk, stir well and cook for a further 2 minutes.

Place the prawns on serving plates and pour over the spicy dressing. Serve at once.

■ COOK'S TIP

Peel onions under cold running water to prevent your eyes watering. It also helps to wrap them and chill them in the refrigerator for 30 minutes before chopping.

■ COOK'S TIP

This dressing can be adapted in a number of ways – omit the coconut milk and add diced, cooked potatoes instead for a dressing to serve with chicken slices or eggs.

43 CURRIED PRAWN RING

Preparation time:
25 minutes, plus chilling time

Cooking time:
about 25 minutes

Serves 4-6

Calories:
360-240 per portion

YOU WILL NEED:
350 g/12 oz long-grain rice
few saffron threads
1 tablespoon sunflower oil
1 tablespoon curry powder
8 spring onions, chopped
1 red pepper, seeded and chopped
50 g/2 oz pine nuts
75 g/3 oz sultanas
225 g/8 oz peeled prawns
FOR THE DRESSING
4 tablespoons olive oil
2 tablespoons white wine vinegar
1 teaspoon dry mustard
1 teaspoon sugar
2 tablespoons chopped coriander leaves

Cook the rice in boiling salted water with the saffron added for 20 minutes until tender. Meanwhile, shake the dressing ingredients in a screw-topped jar to blend.

Drain the rice, place in a bowl and stir in the dressing while still warm. Cool slightly.

Heat the oil in a pan, add the curry powder, spring onions, red pepper, pine nuts and sultanas and cook, stirring, for 1½ minutes. Add to the rice; leave to cool.

Stir in the prawns, then spoon the mixture into a lightly oiled 1.5 litre/2½ pint ring mould, pressing down well. Chill until required, then invert on to a serving plate.

COOK'S TIP

Shake the ring mould gently but firmly to remove the Curried prawn ring without it breaking up. If you like, garnish the centre of the ring with watercress and prawns.

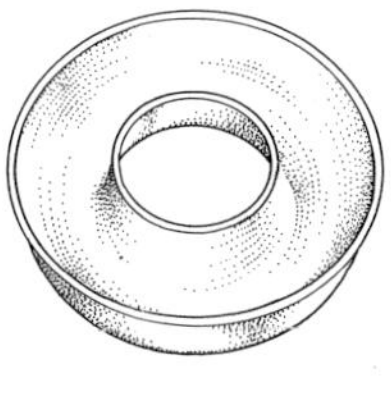

44 BAKED SPICED FISH

Preparation time:
10 minutes, plus overnight marinating time

Cooking time:
30 minutes

Oven temperature:
180C, 350F, gas 4

Serves 4

Calories:
180 per portion with white fish (400 per portion with oily fish)

YOU WILL NEED:
250 ml/8 fl oz natural yogurt
1 onion, chopped
1 garlic clove, chopped
1 teaspoon grated root ginger
1 tablespoon vinegar
1½ teaspoons ground cumin
pinch of chilli powder
1 kg/2 lb whole fish or 675 g/1½ lb fish fillets (see Cook's Tip)
juice of 1 lemon
1 teaspoon salt
FOR THE GARNISH
lemon slices
fresh coriander leaves

Put a quarter of the yogurt, the onion, garlic, ginger, vinegar, cumin and chilli powder in a liquidizer or food processor and blend to a smooth sauce. Add the remaining yogurt.

Score the fish and place in an ovenproof dish. Rub with lemon juice and sprinkle with the salt. Pour over the yogurt marinade, cover and leave to marinate overnight.

Cover the fish with foil and bake for 30 minutes. Serve hot, garnished with lemon slices and coriander leaves.

COOK'S TIP

When selecting the fish for this dish you will find that whole fish give the best results – try bream, snapper or flounder for example. You can use an oily fish such as mackerel but increase the amount of vinegar to 2 tablespoons. If using fillets, select cod or a similar chunky fish, or use fish steaks.

45 SPICY PRAWNS

Preparation time: 8 minutes	YOU WILL NEED: 450 g/1 lb peeled prawns
	1 teaspoon ground coriander
Cooking time: 15-20 minutes	1 heaped tablespoon chopped parsley
	1 egg, beaten
Serves 4-6	40 g/1 ½ oz fresh wholewheat breadcrumbs
Calories: 280-190 per portion	3 tablespoons oil
	2 onions, finely chopped
	1 garlic clove, crushed
	¼ teaspoon chilli powder
	½ teaspoon ground ginger
	¼ teaspoon ground bay leaves
	150 ml/¼ pint hot water
	juice of 1 lemon

Mince the prawns and mix with the coriander and parsley. Divide and shape into walnut-sized balls; dip into the egg and coat in the breadcrumbs. Set aside.

Heat 2 tablespoons of the oil in a frying pan, add the prawn balls and fry until golden. Remove and keep warm. Heat the remaining oil, add the onions and fry until brown. Stir in the garlic, chilli powder, ginger and ground bay leaves and cook, stirring, for about 5 minutes.

Add the hot water, bring to the boil, then simmer for 8-10 minutes. Stir in the lemon juice. Serve the sauce with the prawn balls.

46 MACKEREL ANGOOR

Preparation time: 20 minutes	YOU WILL NEED: 50 g/2 oz butter
Cooking time: 30 minutes	2 whole medium or 4 whole small mackerel, gutted, cleaned and heads removed
Oven temperature: 180C, 350F, gas 4	1 medium onion, finely chopped
	1 garlic clove, crushed
Serves 4	450 g/1 lb green grapes, halved and seeds removed
Calories: 430 per portion	1 teaspoon ground nutmeg
	1 teaspoon chilli powder
	1 teaspoon ground cumin
	salt

Melt the butter in a frying pan and quickly fry the fish for 1 minute on each side. Drain using a slotted fish slice and transfer to a shallow ovenproof dish.

Fry the onion and garlic for 2-3 minutes in the juices in the pan. Reserve 20 grape halves for garnish and chop half the remainder. Add the nutmeg, chilli powder, cumin, chopped grapes, grape halves and salt and fry quickly for a further 2-3 minutes. Pour the mixture evenly over the fish. Cover and bake for 25-30 minutes.

Garnish with the reserved halves of grapes and serve at once.

■ COOK'S TIP

To chop parsley finely, hold the tip of the knife on the board with one hand and move the other end of the knife in arcs over the parsley until it is chopped finely.

■ COOK'S TIP

To prepare the mackerel, cut off the fins with scissors and trim the tail. Cut off the head just below the gills. Slit the fish along the belly, remove the innards, then rinse.

47 CURRIED CRAB

Preparation time:
about 20 minutes

Cooking time:
20 minutes

Serves 6

Calories:
550 per portion

YOU WILL NEED:

1 fresh coconut
75 g/3 oz ghee
1 large onion, sliced
4 garlic cloves, sliced
1 x 7.5 cm/3 inch piece root ginger,
    peeled and thinly sliced
2 teaspoons fenugreek seeds
2 teaspoons peppercorns
2 teaspoons chilli powder
2 teaspoons ground coriander
1 teaspoon turmeric
1 teaspoon salt
450 g/1 lb natural yogurt
300 ml/½ pint milk
450 g/1 lb crab meat

Prepare the coconut as in the Cook's Tip. Heat the ghee, add the onion, garlic and ginger and fry for 5 minutes. Add the fenugreek, peppercorns, chilli powder, coriander, turmeric and salt. Stir well and fry for 2-3 minutes, then add the coconut milk. Mix the yogurt with the milk and slowly stir into the pan. Bring to just below boiling point and simmer for 5-6 minutes.

Add the crab meat and sliced coconut and cook gently for 5 minutes. Serve at once.

48 FISH IN CREAMED CORN

Preparation time:
30 minutes

Cooking time:
35-40 minutes

Oven temperature:
180C, 350F, gas 4

Serves 4

Calories:
290 per portion

YOU WILL NEED:

4 coley fillets, about 175 g/6 oz each
50 g/2 oz butter
1 medium onion, minced
2 garlic cloves, creamed
2 teaspoons cumin seeds, crushed
1 x 30 g/11 oz can creamed sweetcorn,
    or 1 x 300 g/11 oz can sweetcorn
    kernels, drained and liquidized to a
    smooth cream
1 tablespoon chopped fresh coriander
    leaves
salt
2 sprigs fresh coriander leaves, to
    garnish

Wash and pat the fish dry on absorbent kitchen paper, then place in a shallow ovenproof dish.

Melt the butter in a pan over a gentle heat, add the onion, garlic and cumin and fry for 5-7 minutes, stirring occasionally. Add the creamed corn, fresh coriander and salt. Stir thoroughly, then pour the mixture over the fish. Cover and bake for 25-30 minutes. Garnish with the coriander sprigs and serve at once.

◾ COOK'S TIP

Make holes in the eyes of the coconut, drain out the liquid and reserve. Crack open the coconut and cut out the flesh. Thinly slice ¼ of the flesh and blend the remainder in a liquidizer. Add 600 ml/ 1 pint boiling water, stir for 5 minutes then strain through cheesecloth. Mix the liquid from the coconut with the prepared milk.

◾ COOK'S TIP

The sweetness of the corn complements the distinctive taste of the coley in this recipe, though you could try the sauce with a blander-tasting fish such as cod.

49 COCONUT FISH

Preparation time:
10 minutes

Cooking time:
15 minutes

Serves 4

Calories:
450 per portion

YOU WILL NEED:
2 tablespoons oil
4 green chillies, seeded and chopped
2 garlic cloves, chopped
1 x 2.5 cm/1 inch piece root ginger,
*   finely chopped*
100 g/4 oz creamed coconut
1 kg/2 lb thick haddock fillets, skinned
*   and cubed*
salt
juice of 2 lemons

Heat the oil in a large frying pan, add the chillies, garlic and ginger and fry for 3 minutes. Add the creamed coconut and, when bubbling, add the fish and salt to taste. Stir well.

Cook for 3-4 minutes, stirring and breaking up the fish as it cooks. As soon as all the fish is cooked through, pour in the lemon juice, stir well and serve.

50 FRIED PRAWNS AND PEPPER

Preparation time:
15 minutes

Cooking time:
20-25 minutes

Serves 4

Calories:
400 per portion

YOU WILL NEED:
100 g/4 oz butter
1 large onion, finely chopped
2 tablespoons ground coriander
50 g/2 oz desiccated coconut
450 g/1 lb peeled prawns, defrosted if
*   frozen*
1 teaspoon salt
1 teaspoon chilli powder
1/4 teaspoon turmeric
1 large green pepper, seeded and diced

Heat the butter in a large frying pan, add the onion and fry until just soft. Add the coriander and coconut and fry for 2 minutes. Add the prawns and stir-fry for about 5-7 minutes until heated through. Add the remaining ingredients and stir-fry for a further 2-3 minutes. Serve immediately.

■ COOK'S TIP

Coconut is particularly good with fish in this dish which is simple to make and not too chilli hot. Serve it with boiled rice and a lentil dhal (see recipes 175 and 129).

■ COOK'S TIP

Timing is essential when stir-frying. Keep each item moving briskly round the pan to ensure it cooks evenly and absorbs all the flavours.

51   STEAMED MUSSELS

Preparation time:
40 minutes

Cooking time:
10-15 minutes

Serves 6

Calories:
250 per portion

YOU WILL NEED:
1 kg/2¼ lb mussels
100 g/4 oz ghee
1 large onion, chopped
2 garlic cloves, chopped
2 teaspoons desiccated coconut
2 teaspoons salt
1 teaspoon turmeric
1 teaspoon chilli powder
1 teaspoon freshly ground black pepper
150 ml/¼ pint vinegar
450 g/1 lb natural yogurt
2 teaspoons garam masala
juice of 2 lemons

Prepare the fish as in the Cook's Tip. Heat the ghee, add the onion and garlic and fry for 5 minutes. Add the coconut and salt and fry until browned. Add the turmeric, chilli powder and pepper and fry for 1 minute. Add the vinegar and shellfish, cover and bring to the boil; cook for about 5 minutes or until the shells open, then remove from the heat.

Remove the empty half shells and discard. Arrange the remainder in a serving dish. Pour the cooking liquid into a liquidizer or food processor with the yogurt and garam masala and blend for 1 minute. Reheat until hot but not boiling. Pour over the shellfish, sprinkle with lemon juice and serve at once.

52   FISH FRITTERS

Preparation time:
15-20 minutes, plus standing time

Cooking time:
10-15 minutes

Serves 4

Calories:
250 per portion

YOU WILL NEED:
6 tablespoons oil
2 onions, chopped
1 tablespoon ground coriander
3 green chillies, seeded and chopped
1 teaspoon salt
1 teaspoon pepper
675 g/1½ lb cod fillets, skinned and cut
    into small pieces
2 tablespoons finely chopped fresh
    coriander leaves
FOR THE BATTER
100 g/4 oz gram flour or bessan
½ teaspoon chilli powder
½ teaspoon salt
1 egg, beaten
7 tablespoons water

Heat 3 tablespoons of the oil in a pan. Add the onions and fry until just soft. Stir in the coriander, chillies, salt and pepper, then add the fish. Fry for 2 minutes, then cover and cook on a very low heat for 2 minutes. Break up the mixture with a fork and add the chopped coriander. Set aside.

To make the batter, sift the flour, chilli powder and salt into a bowl. Add the egg and water and beat to make a smooth batter. Leave to stand for 30 minutes.

Stir the fish mixture into the batter. Heat the remaining oil in a frying pan and drop in small spoonfuls; fry on both sides until golden. Drain the fritters thoroughly, then serve while still warm.

▉ COOK'S TIP

Scrub the mussels under cold running water and pull away the 'beard'. Soak 30 minutes. Discard any mussels that are not tightly shut or that do not shut quickly when tapped.

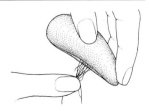

▉ COOK'S TIP

Fresh fish should be cooked as soon as possible after purchase. Its flesh should be firm and its body stiff, the eyes should be protruding and bright, and the scales plentiful and shiny. Smell is, of course, one of the best indicators of freshness: reject any fish that has an unpleasant odour.

Meat Dishes

The meat-eating habits of the Indian population vary enormously: Muslims eat beef and lamb but never pork, but pork is the speciality of Goans from the ex-Portuguese colony. The Parsees are omnivorous, yet the majority of the population is Hindu and largely vegetarian; when Hindus do eat meat it is never beef.

53 KOFTA IN YOGURT

Preparation time:
15 minutes

Cooking time:
about 8-10 minutes

Serves 4

Calories:
400 per portion

YOU WILL NEED:
450 g/1 lb minced beef
75 g/3 oz fresh breadcrumbs
2 green chillies, finely chopped
1 onion, finely chopped
1 x 2.5 cm/1 inch piece root ginger, finely chopped
2 teaspoons ground coriander
salt
1 egg, lightly beaten
oil for frying
450 g/1 lb natural yogurt
2 tablespoons chopped fresh coriander leaves, to garnish

Mix the minced beef with the breadcrumbs, chillies, onion, ginger, ground coriander, salt to taste and egg, blending well. Divide and shape the mixture into walnut sized balls.

Heat the oil in a large pan, add the meat balls and fry until well browned and cooked through. Drain carefully.

Pour the yogurt into a serving bowl and add the meat balls while still hot. Sprinkle with the chopped coriander leaves and serve while still warm.

54 CALCUTTA BEEF CURRY

Preparation time:
about 20 minutes

Cooking time:
about 1³/₄-2¹/₄ hours

Serves 4-6

Calories:
860-570 per portion

YOU WILL NEED:
1 teaspoon salt
2 teaspoons chilli powder
2 teaspoons ground coriander
1 teaspoon freshly ground black pepper
1 ¹/₂ teaspoons turmeric
1 teaspoon ground cumin
1 litre/1 ³/₄ pints milk
1 kg/2-2 ¹/₄ lb braising steak, cubed
100 g/4 oz ghee
2 large onions, thinly sliced
5 garlic cloves, thinly sliced
1 x 7.5 cm/3 inch piece root ginger, peeled and thinly sliced
2 teaspoons garam masala

Place the salt and ground spices except the garam masala, in a large bowl. Mix in a little of the milk to make a paste, then gradually add the remaining millk. Add the beef and turn in the milk and spice mixture until well coated.

Melt the ghee in a large saucepan, add the onions, garlic and ginger and fry gently for 4-5 minutes until soft. Remove the beef from the milk and spice mixture, add it to the pan and fry over a moderate heat, turning the meat to seal.

Increase the heat, add the milk and spice mixture and bring to the boil. Cover, reduce the heat and cook gently for 1¹/₂-2 hours until the beef is tender and the sauce reduced.

Just before serving, sprinkle in the garam masala. Increase the heat and boil off any excess liquid until a thick sauce coats the cubes of beef. Transfer to a serving dish and serve.

▓ COOK'S TIP

Make a large batch of breadcrumbs and freeze them for future use. Reduce a whole loaf to crumbs in a liquidizer, then pack them loosely in freezer bags.

▓ COOK'S TIP

This recipe is more commonly made in Calcutta with lamb or goat meat, but the use of beef enhances the flavour of the sauce.

55 SPICED BEEF IN YOGURT

Preparation time:
15 minutes, plus
overnight marinating
time

Cooking time:
about 1 hour 40
minutes

Serves 4

Calories:
650 per portion

YOU WILL NEED:
450 g/1 lb braising or stewing steak,
  thinly sliced
1 teaspoon salt
300 ml/½ pint natural yogurt
175 g/6 oz ghee
1 large onion, sliced
3 garlic cloves, sliced
1½ teaspoons ground ginger
2 teaspoons ground coriander
2 teaspoons chilli powder
½ teaspoon ground cumin
1½ teaspoons turmeric
1 teaspoon garam masala

Place the beef between 2 sheets of greaseproof paper and beat with a mallet or rolling pin until thin. Rub the beef with the salt, cut into serving-sized pieces, then place in a bowl and cover with the yogurt. Cover and refrigerate overnight.

Melt the ghee in a large saucepan, add the onion and garlic and fry gently for 4-5 minutes until soft. Add the ginger, coriander, chilli powder, cumin, turmeric and garam masala and fry for a further 3 minutes, stirring constantly.

Add the beef and yogurt marinade to the pan, stir well, cover with a tight-fitting lid and simmer for about 1½ hours until the meat is tender. Serve hot.

56 BROCCOLI GOSHT

Preparation time:
30 minutes

Cooking time:
1 hour

Serves 4

Calories:
420 per portion

YOU WILL NEED:
100 g/4 oz hard margarine
1 large onion, finely chopped
2 garlic cloves, creamed
450 g/1 lb braising steak, cut into
  narrow strips
1 tablespoon ground coriander
1 teaspoon garam masala
1 teaspoon chilli powder
1 teaspoon mustard powder
salt
1 x 225 g/8 oz can tomatoes, chopped
  with the juice
225 g/8 oz broccoli spears, washed and
  separated

Melt the margarine in a large saucepan, add the onion and fry until lightly browned. Add the garlic and fry for 1 minute. Add the beef and fry until sealed on all sides. Reduce the heat, then cover and cook the meat in its own juices until tender.

Add the coriander, garam masala, chilli powder, mustard and salt and stir-fry over a low heat for a few seconds. Stir in the tomatoes and cook, uncovered, until almost dry. Add the broccoli and stir-fry for a few minutes. Partly cover the pan and simmer until tender. Transfer to a serving dish and serve at once.

■ COOK'S TIP

This dish from northern India can be made using lamb instead of the beef, if you prefer. Lean lamb fillet would be a good choice.

■ COOK'S TIP

Frozen broccoli can be used instead of fresh. Defrost it completely, then remove any excess liquid by draining thoroughly and patting dry on absorbent paper.

57   BEEF AND PINEAPPLE CURRY

Preparation time:
15 minutes

Cooking time:
about 1 hour 20 minutes

Serves 4

Calories:
350 per portion

YOU WILL NEED:
2 tablespoons oil
450 g/1 lb braising beef, cubed
1 large onion, chopped
2 tablespoons curry powder
450 ml/¾ pint beef stock
150 g/5 oz natural yogurt
1 small pineapple, cut into chunks
desiccated coconut, to garnish

Heat the oil in a large saucepan, add the beef and onion and fry until the meat is brown and the onion is soft. Stir in the curry powder and cook for a further 2 minutes. Add the stock and yogurt, cover and simmer for 45-50 minutes. Add the pineapple and simmer for a further 15 minutes.

Sprinkle coconut over the curry and serve with Plain Boiled Rice (see recipe 182).

58   MINCED BEEF ON SKEWERS

Preparation time:
20 minutes, plus 30 minutes chilling time

Cooking time:
about 15 minutes

Serves 4-6

Calories:
500-360 per portion

YOU WILL NEED:
675 g/1½ lb minced beef
2 large onions, chopped
4 garlic cloves, chopped
75 g/3 oz breadcrumbs
3 tablespoons chopped fresh coriander
  leaves
2 teaspoons garam masala
2 teaspoons black pepper
1½ teaspoons poppy seeds
1½ teaspoons sesame seeds
½ teaspoon chilli powder
1½ teaspoons salt
2 eggs, beaten

Pass the beef, onions and garlic through the finest blade of a mincer, or work in a food processor. Knead well then mix in the remaining ingredients. Chill for 30 minutes.

Press the mixture on to 6 skewers, in sausage shapes about 10 cm/4 inches long (there should be enough mixture to make 12 shapes, 2 on each skewer). Barbecue or grill under or over a moderate heat until cooked, turning frequently. Serve hot.

■ COOK'S TIP

This is a quick, easy-to-prepare curry for the occasions when you want a warming, spicy dish but haven't much time to prepare it. The use of curry powder and canned pineapple chunks makes it fast and simple, and you could use a stock cube to further speed up the preparation.

■ COOK'S TIP

Remove items from skewers with the prongs of a fork. Remember to protect your hand with a double-thick tea-towel if the skewers are hot from the grill or barbecue.

59   GOAN MEAT CURRY

Preparation time:
30 minutes

Cooking time:
about 1 hour

Serves 4-6

Calories:
390-260 per portion

YOU WILL NEED:
50 g/2 oz ghee or 4 tablespoons oil
1 onion, chopped
5 garlic cloves, chopped
450 g/1 lb lean beef or lamb, cubed
5 garlic cloves, ground to a paste
25 g/1 oz root ginger, peeled and ground
    to a paste
3 green chillies, seeded and very finely
    chopped
½ teaspoon turmeric
2 teaspoons aniseed powder
salt
40 g/1½ oz creamed coconut
about 250 ml/8 fl oz water
2-3 sprigs fresh coriander leaves,
    chopped

Heat the ghee or oil in a large pan, add the onion and chopped garlic and fry until lightly browned. Add the meat, garlic and ginger pastes, chillies and turmeric and mix well. Fry for 6-7 minutes until the meat is dry. Sprinkle with the aniseed powder, add salt to taste, then stir in the creamed coconut. Fry for 1-2 minutes. Add the water and coriander leaves. Cover and cook gently for 30-40 minutes until the meat is tender. Serve at once.

60   CORIANDER BEEF WITH AUBERGINE

Preparation time:
20 minutes

Cooking time:
about 2¼ hours

Serves 6

Calories:
500 per portion

YOU WILL NEED:
75 ml/3 fl oz oil
2 onions, finely sliced
1 x 2.5 cm/1 inch piece root ginger,
    chopped
3 garlic cloves, chopped
3 tablespoons ground coriander
½ teaspoon hot chilli powder
1 kg/2 lb lean boneless beef, cut into
    4 cm/1½ inch cubes
475 ml/16 fl oz beef stock
1 large aubergine, cut into 4 cm/1½ inch
    cubes
675 g/1½ lb tomatoes, chopped
1 x 400 g/14 oz can chick peas, drained
salt and pepper
1 teaspoon garam masala

Heat the oil, add the onion and cook for 0 minutes until tender. Add the ginger, garlic, coriander and chilli powder, then cook for 2 minutes. Stir in the beef and brown for 5 minutes, turning frequently.

   Add the stock, bring to the boil, reduce the heat, cover and simmer for 1½ hours.

   Stir in the aubergine, cover and simmer for 20 minutes. Add the tomatoes and chick peas, cover and simmer for a further 10 minutes, then season to taste with salt and pepper. Stir in the garam masalla and serve at once.

■ COOK'S TIP

*Aniseed powder imparts a
subtle and delicate flavour to
this dish. Whole aniseed is
delicious with carrots and
other cooked vegetables.*

■ COOK'S TIP

*Sprinkling aubergine with salt
draws out any bitter juices
and prevents the aubergine
absorbing too much oil.
Rinse thoroughly or the cubes
will taste salty.*

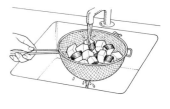

61 BRINJAL CUTLETS

Preparation time:
15 minutes

Cooking time:
about 1 hour

Serves 4

Calories:
380 per portion

YOU WILL NEED:
2 large aubergines
salt
3 tablespoons oil
1 onion, finely chopped
1 garlic clove, finely chopped
2 green chillies, seeded and finely
    chopped
1 teaspoon turmeric
450 g/1 lb minced beef
1 egg, lightly beaten
2-3 tablespoons fresh breadcrumbs

Cook the aubergines in boiling salted water for 15 minutes or until almost tender. Drain thoroughly and cool.

Heat the oil in a pan, add the onion and fry until golden. Add the garlic, chillies and turmeric and fry for 2 minutes. Add the mince and cook, stirring, until brown all over. Add salt to taste and cook gently for 20 minutes, until the meat is tender.

Cut the aubergines in half lengthways. Carefully scoop out the pulp, add it to the meat mixture and mix well. Check the seasoning. Fill the aubergine shells with the mixture, brush with egg and cover with breadcrumbs. Cook under a moderate grill for 4-5 minutes until golden.

62 CHILLI FRY

Preparation time:
15 minutes

Cooking time:
about 20-25 minutes

Serves 4

Calories:
370 per portion

YOU WILL NEED:
4 tablespoons oil
1 large onion, finely chopped
1/2 teaspoon ground coriander
1/2 teaspoon turmeric
1 x 2.5 cm/1 inch piece root ginger,
    finely chopped
1 chilli, chopped
450 g/1 lb frying steak, cut into strips
    about 2.5 x 1 cm/1 x 1/2 inch
1 green or red pepper, cored, seeded and
    chopped
2 tomatoes, quartered
juice of 1 lemon
salt

Heat the oil, add the onion and fry until soft. Add the coriander, turmeric, ginger and chilli and fry over a low heat for 5 minutes.

Add the steak, increase the heat and cook, stirring, until browned all over. Add the pepper, cover and simmer gently for 5-10 minutes, until the meat is tender. Add the tomatoes, lemon juice and salt to taste. Cook, uncovered, for 2-3 minutes. Serve at once.

■ COOK'S TIP

To scoop the flesh from the aubergine, cut around the edge of the aubergine between skin and pulp, leaving a narrow margin of flesh adhering to the skin.

Make criss-cross cuts over the surface before scooping out the pulp.

■ COOK'S TIP

When cooked this dish should be rather dry, so remove the lid for the last part of the cooking time to ensure that any juices are driven off with the heat.

63 TOMATAR GOSHT

Preparation time:
20 minutes

Cooking time:
1 hour 10 minutes

Serves 4-6

Calories:
360-240 per portion

YOU WILL NEED:
50 g/2 oz ghee or 4 tablespoons oil
1 onion, chopped
25 g/1 oz fresh root ginger, peeled and crushed
4-5 garlic cloves, crushed
½ teaspoon turmeric
1 teaspoon ground coriander
1½ teaspoons ground cumin
450 g/1 lb braising steak or leg of lamb, cubed
salt
1-2 green chillies, seeded and very finely chopped, or 1 teaspoon chilli powder
1 x 400 g/14 oz can tomatoes
2-3 sprigs of coriander leaves, chopped

Heat the ghee or oil in a pan and fry the onion until browned. Add the ginger, garlic, turmeric, coriander, cumin, meat and salt to taste. Mix together well, then cover and cook gently for 10-12 minutes. Add the chillies or chilli powder, tomatoes and coriander leaves. Cover and cook for a further 50 minutes. Serve hot.

64 BEEF CURRY ALL IN ONE

Preparation time:
25 minutes

Cooking time:
1-1¼ hours

Oven temperature:
180C, 350F, gas 4

Serves 4

Calories:
380 per portion

YOU WILL NEED:
750 g/1½ lb braising steak, cubed
2 large onions, finely chopped
2 garlic cloves, crushed
1 x 50 g/2 oz piece root ginger, peeled and chopped
2 tablespoons ground coriander
1 teaspoon ground cardamom
1 teaspoon chilli powder
1 teaspoon ground nutmeg
2 teaspoons sugar
1 teaspoon salt
120 ml/4 fl oz oil
1 x 400 g/14 oz can tomatoes, chopped with the juice

Place the beef in an ovenproof casserole dish. Mix together all the remaining ingredients in a bowl and stir well. Pour the mixture evenly over the meat. Cover and bake for 1-1¼ hours, stirring once or twice during the cooking time. Serve at once.

■ COOK'S TIP

The colour of fat varies from one type of animal to another. For instance, grass-fed beef has yellower fat than that of barley-fed beef, which has whiter fat and paler red meat.

■ COOK'S TIP

If you prefer a milder garlic taste, cut the clove in half and remove the pale green central shoot before preparing the remaining flesh.

65 ALOO 'CHOPS'

Preparation time:
25 minutes

Cooking time:
about 1 hour 10 minutes

Serves 4

Calories:
580 per portion

YOU WILL NEED:
3 tablespoons oil
1 large onion, finely chopped
1 x 1 cm/½ inch piece root ginger, finely chopped
1 teaspoon ground coriander seeds
225 g/8 oz minced beef
1 tablespoon raisins
salt
1 tablespoon finely chopped coriander
1 kg/2 lb potatoes, boiled and mashed with a little milk and salt
flour for coating
oil for shallow frying

Heat the oil in a frying pan, add the onion and ginger and fry until golden. Add the ground coriander and minced beef and fry until brown. Add the raisins and salt to taste and simmer for about 20 minutes until the meat is cooked. Spoon out any fat in the pan. Stir in the chopped coriander and leave to cool.

Divide the mashed potato into 8 portions. With well-floured hands, flatten a portion on one palm, put 3 teaspoons of the meat mixture in the centre and fold the potato over it. Form gently into a round patty shape.

Dip the 'chops' lightly in flour and shallow fry a few at a time in hot oil, until crisp and golden, turning carefully to brown the underside. Serve at once.

66 BEEF CURRY WITH POTATOES

Preparation time:
20 minutes

Cooking time:
about 1½ -1¾ hours

Serves 4

Calories:
540 per portion

YOU WILL NEED:
4 tablespoons oil
2 onions, finely chopped
2 garlic cloves, chopped
1 teaspoon chilli powder
1 tablespoon ground cumin
1½ tablespoons ground coriander
1 x 2.5 cm/1 inch piece root ginger, finely chopped
675 g/1½ lb stewing steak, cubed
2 tablespoons tomato purée
salt
350 g/12 oz new potatoes, scraped and halved if large
4 green chillies

Heat the oil in a large pan, add the onions and fry until lightly coloured. Add the garlic, chilli powder, cumin, coriander and ginger and cook gently for 5 minutes, stirring occasionally.

Add the beef and cook, stirring, until browned all over. Add the tomato purée, salt to taste and just enough water to cover the meat; stir very well. Bring to the boil, cover and simmer for about 1 hour or until the meat is almost tender. Add the potatoes and whole chillies and simmer until the potatoes are cooked.

■ COOK'S TIP

Use old potatoes for mashing. Take care not to overcook them, and make sure you drain them properly after boiling or the end result will be sloppy.

■ COOK'S TIP

Leftover amounts of tomato purée from a tin can be frozen in an ice-cube tray and stored for further use.

67 BEEF IN PEANUT SAUCE

Preparation time:
20 minutes

Cooking time:
about 1-1¼ hours

Serves 4

Calories:
460 per portion

YOU WILL NEED:
450 g/1 lb braising steak, cubed
1 medium onion, roughly chopped
50 ml/2 fl oz oil
300 ml/½ pint water
100 g/4 oz fresh, unroasted peanuts,
    finely ground
2 tomatoes, skinned and roughly
    chopped
1 teaspoon chilli powder
1 teaspoon turmeric
salt

Place all the ingredients in a large saucepan and mix thoroughly over a medium heat. Bring to the boil, stirring occasionally. Cover the pan, reduce the heat and simmer for about 45 minutes until the meat is tender. Remove the lid for the last 10 minutes and continue cooking until the sauce has thickened.

68 KOFTA CURRY

Preparation time:
30 minutes

Cooking time:
45 minutes

Serves 4

Calories:
370 per portion

YOU WILL NEED:
3 onions, sliced
2 garlic cloves
2 green chillies
1 x 3.5 cm/1½ inch piece root ginger
25 g/1 oz fresh coriander leaves
25 g/1 oz fresh mint leaves
2 teaspoons salt
450 g/1 lb minced beef
4 tablespoons oil
1 teaspoon chilli powder
1 teaspoon ground cumin
1 tablespoon ground coriander
6 curry leaves
25 g/1 oz tomato purée, diluted in
    300 ml/½ pint water

Place 1 onion, 1 garlic clove, 2 chillies, 1 cm/½ inch piece ginger, coriander leaves, mint and half the salt in a food processor or liquidizer and work to a paste. Mix with the minced beef, roll into walnut-sized balls and fry lightly in 3 tablespoons of the oil. Drain on absorbent kitchen paper and set aside.

Heat the remaining oil in the pan, add the remaining onions and fry until golden. Crush the remaining garlic and chop the remaining ginger. Add to the pan with the chilli powder, cumin, ground coriander and 1 tablespoon water. Fry, stirring, for 2 minutes. Add the curry leaves and fry for 30 seconds, then stir in the tomato paste and remaining salt. Simmer for 10 minutes. Slip the meat balls into the pan and simmer for 30 minutes. Garnish with mint leaves, if liked, and serve.

▨ COOK'S TIP

Unskinned peanuts should be used in this recipe. However, if you prefer to remove the skins, rub them off in a clean cloth.

▨ COOK'S TIP

In India, koftas (meat balls) are a popular way of cooking mince. There are a variety of sauces to serve them with – try the version with yogurt (recipe 53), for example.

69 BHOLAR GOSHT

Preparation time:
25-30 minutes

Cooking time:
35-40 minutes

Serves 4

Calories:
410 per portion

YOU WILL NEED:
50 g/2 oz butter
450 g/1 lb braising steak, cut into
    narrow strips about 5 cm/2 inches
    long
1 medium onion, chopped
50 g/2 oz raisins
1 large green pepper, seeded and cut
    into strips
50 g/2 oz desiccated coconut
1 teaspoon chilli powder
1 teaspoon garam masala
1 teaspoon ground cinnamon
1 teaspoon salt

Heat the butter in a large frying pan. Add the beef, onion and raisins and stir-fry for about 5 minutes. Cover and cook over a low heat for 30-35 minutes until the meat is tender and there is no liquid left in the pan. Add the remaining ingredients and stir-fry for a further 2-3 minutes. The finished dish should be dry and the green pepper crunchy.

70 VEGETABLE KHEEMA

Preparation time:
15 minutes

Cooking time:
about 20 minutes

Serves 4

Calories:
500 per portion

YOU WILL NEED:
4 tablespoons oil
2 onions, chopped
2 teaspoons ground coriander
½ teaspoon turmeric
1 x 2.5 cm/1 inch piece root ginger,
    finely chopped
1 heaped teaspoon garam masala
450 g/1 lb minced beef
225 g/8 oz small potatoes, quartered
salt
450 g/1 lb shelled peas

Heat the oil, add the onions and cook until soft. Add the spices and fry for 5 minutes over a low heat. Stir in the minced beef and cook over a high heat until very well browned.

Lower the heat and add the potatoes and salt to taste. Cover and cook gently for 5 minutes, then add the peas. Continue cooking until the peas and potatoes are tender. Serve hot.

▆ COOK'S TIP

This recipe for beef in pepper is best served simply with Plain Boiled Rice (recipe 182), Poppadoms (recipe 188) and unsweetened natural yogurt.

▆ COOK'S TIP

Use rinsed pea pods to make vegetable stock. Place in a pan with about 1.2 litres/2 pints water, a carrot, sliced onion and bouquet garni, bring to the boil, then simmer 1 hour.

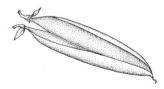

71   DRY LAMB CURRY

Preparation time:
10-15 minutes

Cooking time:
about 50 minutes

Serves 4

Calories:
450 per portion

YOU WILL NEED:

3 tablespoons oil

225 g/8 oz onions, finely chopped

6 cloves

6 cardamoms

1 x 2.5 cm/1 inch piece cinnamon stick

2 green chillies, finely chopped

675 g/1½ lb boned leg of lamb, cut into
  strips

2 teaspoons ground coriander

1 teaspoon ground cumin

300 g/10 oz natural yogurt

2 tablespoons chopped fresh coriander
  leaves

3 curry leaves

salt

1 teaspoon garam masala

Heat the oil in a pan, add the onions and fry until soft. Add the cloves, cardamoms and cinnamon and fry for 1 minute, then add the chillies and lamb. Fry for a further 10 minutes, turning the lamb to brown on all sides.

Add the remaining ingredients, except the garam masala, seasoning with salt to taste. Stir well, bring to simmering point and cook, uncovered, for 40 minutes until the meat is tender and the liquid has evaporated. Stir in the garam masala and serve.

72   LAMB AND LEEK CURRY

Preparation time:
25 minutes

Cooking time:
1½ hours

Oven temperature:
180C, 350F, gas 4

Serves 4

Calories:
520 per portion

YOU WILL NEED:

750 g/1½ lb lamb, cubed

1 large onion, finely chopped

2 garlic cloves, crushed

50 g/2 oz fresh ginger, chopped

150 ml/¼ pint natural yogurt

1 tablespoon plain flour

1 x 225 g/8 oz can tomatoes, chopped
  with the juice

50 ml/2 fl oz oil

1 tablespoon garam masala

1 teaspoon chilli powder

2 teaspoons sugar

2 teaspoons salt

150 ml/¼ pint water

450 g/1 lb leeks, trimmed and cut into
  2.5 cm/1 inch pieces

Place the lamb in a large ovenproof dish. Mix together the remaining ingredients except the leeks in a bowl and pour the mixture evenly over the meat. Cover and bake for 1 hour, stirring once or twice during cooking.

Add the prepared leeks to the casserole and gently stir to cover the leeks with the sauce. Cook for a further 30 minutes, skimming off any excess fat before serving.

▨ COOK'S TIP

Curry making is easy if, before starting to cook, you assemble the ingredients: measure out spices and seasonings into separate piles; chop or slice other foods.

▨ COOK'S TIP

Leeks must be washed very carefully to remove all grit. Cut off the roots and trim the green leaves to within about 2.5 cm/1 inch of the top of the white part. Make a *lengthways slit down one side of the leek and wash under cold running water, rinsing between layers while keeping the shape of the leek intact.*

73 ROYAL LAMB CURRY

Preparation time:
15 minutes, plus 2
hours marinating
time

Cooking time:
about 1¼ hours

Serves 6

Calories:
600 per portion

YOU WILL NEED:
1 kg/2 lb boneless lamb, cubed
juice of 1 lemon
225 g/8 oz natural yogurt
75 g/3 oz ghee
2 onions, sliced
4 garlic cloves, sliced
1 x 2.5 cm/1 inch piece root ginger, sliced
1 x 7.5 cm/3 inch piece cinnamon stick
10 cloves
10 cardamoms
2 teaspoons ground coriander
2 teaspoons ground cumin
2 teaspoons chilli powder
1 teaspoon turmeric
salt and pepper
100 g/4 oz blanched almonds
50 g/2 oz shelled pistachios
150 ml/¼ pint single cream

Mix the lamb with the lemon juice and yogurt and leave to marinate for 2 hours.

Heat the ghee, add the onions, garlic and ginger and fry for 5 minutes. Add the cinnamon, cloves and cardamoms; fry for 1 minute. Add the remaining spices and salt and pepper and cook for 2-3 minutes. Add the lamb and marinade, then stir in 300 ml/½ pint boiling water. Stir in half of the almonds, cover and simmer for 50 minutes.

Add the remaining almonds, pistachios and cream and simmer for 5-10 minutes without boiling. Serve hot.

COOK'S TIP

Varak or silver leaf is often used to decorate this rich and exotic curry. It is safe to eat and aluminium foil should not be used as a substitute.

74 BOTI KEBABS

Preparation time:
20 minutes, plus at
least 15-20 minutes
marinating time

Cooking time:
7-10 minutes

Serves 4-6

Calories:
240-160 per portion

YOU WILL NEED:
25 g/1 oz root ginger, peeled and ground
to a paste, or 2 teaspoons ground
ginger
1 teaspoon garlic powder or purée
450 g/1 lb boned leg or shoulder of
lamb, cut into thin 2.5 cm/1 inch
lengths
1½ teaspoons chilli powder
2 tablespoons vinegar
1 teaspoon freshly ground black pepper
salt
juice of 1 lemon
a little oil

Mix the ginger and garlic with the meat in a large bowl. Sprinkle with the chilli powder, vinegar, pepper and salt to taste. Mix well to coat the meat with all the spices. Add the lemon juice, cover and set aside for at least 15-20 minutes to marinate. For a better result leave to marinate for 3-4 hours or overnight.

Before cooking, stir the marinated ingredients again, then thread the pieces of meat on to skewers. Place the kebabs in a flameproof tray and cook under a moderate grill for about 4-5 minutes on each side, brushing them with a little oil occasionally.

COOK'S TIP

These kebabs can also be cooked in the oven. Place on a wire rack in a baking tray and bake at 180C, 350F, gas 4, for 15-20 minutes, turning occasionally.

75 HURRY CURRY

Preparation time:
15 minutes, plus
overnight standing time

Cooking time:
about 1½ hours

Serves 4

Calories:
360 per portion

YOU WILL NEED:
450 g/1 lb stewing lamb, beef or pork,
*   cubed*
450 g/1 lb onions, finely chopped
1 x 2.5 cm/1 inch piece cinnamon stick
6 cloves
1 tablespoon ground coriander seeds
½ teaspoon ground cumin seeds
½ teaspoon turmeric
1 teaspoon chilli powder
1 x 2.5 cm/1 inch piece root ginger,
*   finely chopped*
1 tablespoon tomato purée
3 tablespoons oil
salt
225 g/8 oz small new potatoes
*   (optional)*

Place all the ingredients except the potatoes, if using, in a pan, seasoning with salt to taste. Stir well. The mixture should be moist; add an extra tablespoon of oil if necessary. Cover the pan tightly and leave overnight in the refrigerator.

Cook over a moderately high heat until the mixture starts to fry briskly. Stir well, then lower the heat and simmer for about 1½ hours until the meat is tender. Add the potatoes, if using, about 20 minutes before the end of the cooking time.

76 KHEEMA DO PYAZA

Preparation time:
20 minutes

Cooking time:
about 50 minutes

Serves 4

Calories:
500 per portion

YOU WILL NEED:
450 g/1 lb onions
4 tablespoons oil
1 x 2.5 cm/1 inch piece root ginger,
*   peeled and chopped*
1 garlic clove, finely chopped
2 green chillies, finely chopped
1 teaspoon turmeric
1 teaspoon ground coriander seeds
1 teaspoon ground cumin seeds
750 g/1½ lb minced lamb
150 g/5 oz natural yogurt
1 x 227 g/8 oz can tomatoes
salt

Finely chop 350 g/12 oz of the onions and thinly slice the remainder.

Heat 2 tablespoons of the oil in a pan, add the chopped onion and fry until golden. Add the ginger, garlic, chillies and spices and fry for 2 minutes. Add the minced lamb and cook, stirring to break it up, until well browned. Stir in the yogurt, a spoonful at a time, until it is absorbed, then add the tomatoes with their juice, and salt to taste. Bring to the boil, stir well, cover and simmer for 20 minutes until the meat is cooked.

Meanwhile, fry the sliced onions in the remaining oil until brown and crisp.

Transfer the meat mixture to a warmed serving dish and sprinkle with the fried onion.

COOK'S TIP

Keep a cinnamon stick in a jar of caster sugar, and use the resulting flavoured sugar on melon, apple dishes, or hot buttered toast.

COOK'S TIP

You may prefer to buy a lean piece of lamb and mince it yourself in a food processor or mincer. Always use mince the day it is bought or prepared.

77　MINTY LAMB CURRY

Preparation time:
25 minutes

Cooking time:
about 1-1½ hours

Serves 4

Calories:
400 per portion

YOU WILL NEED:
100 g/4 oz butter
1 large onion, finely chopped
1 tablespoon ground coriander
1 teaspoon ground cardamom
1 teaspoon fennel seeds, crushed
1 x 400 g/14 oz can tomatoes, chopped
*   with the juice*
1 teaspoon salt
1 teaspoon sugar
1 tablespoon mint sauce
150 ml/¼ pint water
450 g/1 lb lamb, cubed
sprigs of fresh mint, to garnish

Melt the butter in a large saucepan, add the onion and fry until golden. Add the coriander, cardamom and fennel seeds and fry for a few seconds, stirring constantly to prevent burning. Add the tomatoes, salt, sugar and mint sauce and cook for 5 minutes. Stir in the water and meat and mix well with the sauce. Cover and cook for about 1-1½ hours over a low heat until the meat is tender. Serve at once.

78　LAMB KEBABS

Preparation time:
10 minutes, plus
overnight chilling time

Cooking time:
10 minutes

Serves 4

Calories:
450 per portion

YOU WILL NEED:
300 g/10 oz natural yogurt
1 tablespoon ground coriander
½ teaspoon chilli powder
1 tablespoon oil
salt
675 g/1½ lb boned leg of lamb, cubed
4 onions
2 red peppers
4 tomatoes
2 tablespoons finely chopped fresh
*   coriander leaves*

Put the yogurt, coriander, chilli powder, oil and salt to taste in a large bowl. Add the meat, mix well, cover and chill overnight in the refrigerator.

Cut the onion into quarters and separate the layers. Core and seed the peppers and cut into squares and cut the tomatoes in half.

Thread the onion, lamb and red pepper alternately on to 8 skewers, beginning and ending each kebab with a tomato half. Cook under a hot grill for about 10 minutes, turning frequently and basting with any remaining marinade as necessary. Sprinkle with chopped coriander to serve.

■ COOK'S TIP

The flesh of very young lamb is light pink, the fat is creamy-white and the knuckle bones have a bluish tinge. The flesh is darker coloured, varying from light to dark red, in an older animal.

■ COOK'S TIP

Serve the kebabs with a finger bowl – make it effective by adding a few drops of lemon juice and make it look decorative by floating a few flower heads on the surface.

79 DRY SPICED LAMB CHOPS

Preparation time:
10 minutes, plus 1-2
hours marinating time

Cooking time:
about 15 minutes

Serves 4-6

Calories:
450-300 per portion

YOU WILL NEED:
8 chump or loin lamb chops
about ½ teaspoon chilli powder
2 teaspoons ground ginger
2 teaspoons garlic powder
freshly ground black pepper
salt
150 g/5 oz natural yogurt
about 1 tablespoon oil
FOR THE GARNISH
wedges of lemon or lime
fried onion rings

Place the chops in a large bowl and sprinkle over the chilli
powder, ginger, garlic powder, pepper and salt to taste. Add
the yogurt, mix well, cover and leave to marinate for
1-2 hours.

Pour the oil on to the marinated chops and mix again
thoroughly. Lift the chops out and cook under a moderate grill
for 4-6 minutes on each side. Serve hot, garnished with lemon
or lime and onion rings.

80 APRICOT AND LAMB CURRY

Preparation time:
20 minutes, plus
overnight soaking

Cooking time:
1 hour

Serves 4

Calories:
700 per portion

YOU WILL NEED:
4 onions, 2 quartered and 2 chopped
2 garlic cloves
½ -1 teaspoon small dried red chillies
50 g/2 oz blanched almonds
1 tablespoon ground coriander
3 tablespoons oil
1 x 5 cm/2 inch piece cinnamon stick
6 cardamoms
8 cloves
675 g/1½ lb boned leg of lamb, cubed
275 g/10 oz natural yogurt
225 g/8 oz dried apricots, soaked
  overnight
salt
1 tablespoon chopped mint leaves

Put the quartered onions, garlic, chillies, almonds and coriander in a liquidizer or food processor and work to a smooth
paste.

Heat the oil, add the cinnamon, cardamoms and cloves
and fry for a few seconds. When they change colour remove
and discard. Add the remaining onions to the pan and fry until
soft. Add the prepared paste and fry for 3-4 minutes. Add the
lamb and fry, stirring for 5 minutes. Stir in the yogurt, a
spoonful at a time, then the drained apricots and salt to taste.
Simmer, partially covered, for 40 minutes until tender. Stir in
the mint and serve at once.

◼ COOK'S TIP

*An alternative way to cook
the chops is to heat 1
tablespoon oil in a large pan,
add 1 chopped onion and fry
until tender. Add the
marinated meat and any*
*marinade, cover and cook
gently for 40-50 minutes until
the chops are cooked and the
mixture is dry.*

◼ COOK'S TIP

*Apricots go especially well
with lamb but must be of the
best quality with a bright
colour and sharp taste; pallid
sweet fruit will add nothing
to the dish.*

81 MALABAR LAMB CURRY

Preparation time:
10 minutes

Cooking time:
1 hour

Serves 4

Calories:
470 per portion

YOU WILL NEED:
3 tablespoons oil or ghee
2 onions, finely chopped
1 teaspoon turmeric
1 tablespoon ground coriander
1 teaspoon ground cumin
2 teaspoons chilli powder
½ teaspoon ground cloves
12 curry leaves
675 g/1½ lb boned leg of lamb, cubed
1 tablespoon coarsely grated fresh
    coconut
300 ml/½ pint water
1 teaspoon salt

Heat the oil or ghee in a pan, add the onions and fry until golden. Stir in the turmeric, coriander, cumin, chilli powder, cloves and curry leaves and fry for 1-2 minutes.

Add the meat and coconut and fry, stirring, until well browned. Pour in the water and add the salt. Cover and simmer for 45 minutes or until the lamb is tender. Turn on to a warmed serving dish and serve hot.

82 LAMB CURRY IN THE OVEN

Preparation time:
20-25 minutes

Cooking time:
about 1¼ hours

Oven temperature:
180C, 350F, gas 4

Serves 4

Calories:
460 per portion

YOU WILL NEED:
750 g/1½ lb lamb, cubed
1 large onion, finely chopped
2 garlic cloves, crushed
50 ml/2 fl oz oil
1 tablespoon ground coriander
1 tablespoon mustard powder
1 teaspoon ground cardamom
1 teaspoon ground nutmeg
1 teaspoon chilli powder
2 teaspoons salt
2 teaspoons sugar
1 x 400 g/14 oz can tomatoes, chopped
    with the juice

Place the meat in an ovenproof casserole dish. Mix the remaining ingredients in a bowl and stir well, then pour the mixture evenly over the meat. Cover and bake for about 1¼ hours, stirring once during cooking.

Skim off any excess fat and serve at once.

■ COOK'S TIP

Apricot Chutney (recipe 211) and Bertha's Chutney (recipe 209) go well with this dish. Serve it with a rice dish, Poppadoms (recipe 188) and a green salad as well.

■ COOK'S TIP

To make onion butter, cream 100 g/4 oz butter with 2 tablespoons finely chopped or grated onion. Chill in the refrigerator. Serve spread on hot bread, with baked *potatoes, fish and meats, pasta or vegetables.*

83 MEAT WITH SPINACH

Preparation time:
30 minutes

Cooking time:
50 minutes-1 hour
10 minutes

Serves 4-6

Calories:
340-230 per portion

YOU WILL NEED:

2 x 225 g/8 oz packets frozen leaf
    spinach, defrosted and chopped
50 g/2 oz ghee
1 small onion, sliced
40 g/1½ oz root ginger, peeled and
    crushed
5 garlic cloves, crushed
1 teaspoon chilli powder
1 teaspoon ground coriander
1 teaspoon ground cumin
4 fresh tomatoes, peeled and chopped
½ teaspoon turmeric
salt
450 g/1 lb boned leg or shoulder of
    lamb, cubed
200 ml/⅓ pint water

Either sieve or blend the spinach to make a purée and set aside.

Heat the ghee in a large pan and fry the onion until golden. Add the ginger, garlic, chilli powder, coriander and cumin and fry gently for 1-2 minutes. Add the tomatoes, turmeric and salt to taste. Continue frying gently for 10-15 minutes, until the ghee separates and rises to the surface. Add the meat and cook for 7 minutes, or until the meat is dry.

Add the water, cover and cook gently for 30-40 minutes. After about 15 minutes cooking time and when the sauce has been reduced by half, add the spinach purée. Stir well, cover and simmer gently.

■ COOK'S TIP

You can use 1 kg/2 lb chopped fresh spinach if you prefer. Place it in a pan with the water that clings to the leaves after washing, and cook for 10 minutes. Strain it

before sieving or blending it to make a purée, then continue with the recipe as above.

84 LAMB WITH EXTRA ONIONS

Preparation time:
15 minutes

Cooking time:
about 1-1¼ hours

Serves 4-6

Calories:
700-480 per portion

YOU WILL NEED:

675 g/1½ lb boneless shoulder of lamb,
    cubed
5 large onions
100 g/4 oz ghee
6 garlic cloves, peeled
1 x 2.5 cm/1 inch piece root ginger
1 tablespoon chilli powder
2 teaspoons ground coriander
2 teaspoons ground cumin
2 teaspoons black pepper
1½ teaspoons turmeric
2 teaspoons salt
350 g/12 oz natural yogurt
300 ml/½ pint beef stock
6 green chillies, chopped
1 tablespoon fenugreek seeds
2 tablespoons chopped fresh mint

Place the lamb in a bowl. Purée 1 onion in a liquidizer or food processor and add to the lamb.

Heat the ghee, add the lamb mixture and fry on all sides. Slice the remaining onions, garlic and peeled ginger. Remove the lamb with a slotted spoon and set aside. Add the sliced onions, garlic and ginger and fry gently for 4-5 minutes. Meanwhile, mix the ground spices and salt with the yogurt. Add to the pan, increase the heat and add the lamb, stirring constantly. Add the stock, bring to the boil, cover and simmer for 40 minutes.

Add the chillies, fenugreek and mint and simmer for a further 5-10 minutes. Serve hot.

■ COOK'S TIP

Shoulder of lamb is a very tender and sweet joint, but it can be fatty. Ask your butcher to bone it, but to leave it untied so you can remove any excess fat before dicing it.

85 LAMB CURRY WITH YOGURT

Preparation time:
15 minutes

Cooking time:
about 1¼ hours

Serves 4

Calories:
450 per portion

YOU WILL NEED:
4 tablespoons oil
3 onions, chopped
6 cardamoms
1 x 5 cm/2 inch piece cinnamon stick
1½ tablespoons ground coriander
2 tablespoons ground cumin
½ teaspoon turmeric
½ teaspoon ground cloves
1-2 teaspoons chilli powder
½ teaspoon grated nutmeg
2 tablespoons water
1 tablespoon paprika
300 g/10 oz natural yogurt
675 g/1½ lb boned leg of lamb, cubed
1 large tomato, skinned and chopped
salt

Heat the oil in a large pan, add the onions, cardamoms and cinnamon and fry until the onions are golden. Stir in the coriander, cumin, turmeric, cloves, chilli powder and nutmeg. Fry until dry, then add the water and cook, stirring, for 5 minutes, adding a little more water if needed.

Add the paprika and slowly stir in the yogurt. Add the lamb, tomato and salt to taste and mix well. Bring to simmering point, cover and cook for 1 hour or until the meat is tender.

86 RICE AND LAMB TARI

Preparation time:
20 minutes, plus marinating time

Cooking time:
1¼ hours

Oven temperature:
190C, 375F, gas 5

Serves 4-6

Calories:
800-540 per portion

YOU WILL NEED:
50 g/2 oz root ginger, chopped
40 g/1½ oz coriander leaves and stems
4 garlic cloves
275 g/10 oz natural yogurt
salt
450 g/1 lb boned leg of lamb, cubed
50 g/2 oz butter or ghee
1 x 5 cm/2 inch piece cinnamon stick
4 cloves
4 cardamoms
4 onions, finely chopped
450 g/1 lb Basmati rice, washed, soaked and drained

Put the ginger, coriander and garlic in a liquidizer or food processor and work to a paste. Mix with the yogurt, 1 teaspoon salt and lamb and leave for 2 hours.

Heat the butter or ghee in a pan and fry the cinnamon, cloves and cardamoms for a few seconds. Add the onions and fry gently until golden. Add the lamb and marinade, cover and simmer for 30 minutes.

Meanwhile, parboil the rice in boiling salted water for 3 minutes; drain. Mix the rice and meat curry together and place in a casserole. Cover tightly and bake for 30 minutes. Serve hot.

■ COOK'S TIP

To skin tomatoes, place them in a bowl of boiling water for 1 minute. Drain, then plunge into cold water and pull off the skin with a pointed knife.

■ COOK'S TIP

Basmati is the best rice to use in savoury dishes because of its distinct aroma and slightly nutty flavour. The flavour of American long-grain rice is not as good.

87 ROGHAN GHOSHT

Preparation time:
20 minutes

Cooking time:
about 1¼ hours

Serves 4

Calories:
650 per portion

YOU WILL NEED:
4 tablespoons oil
2 onions, finely chopped
675 g/1½ lb boned leg of lamb, cubed
300 g/10 oz natural yogurt
2 garlic cloves
1 x 2.5 cm/1 inch piece root ginger
2 green chillies
1 tablespoon coriander seeds
1 teaspoon cumin seeds
1 teaspoon chopped fresh mint leaves
1 teaspoon chopped coriander leaves
6 cardamoms
6 cloves
1 x 2.5 cm/1 inch piece cinnamon stick
salt
100 g/4 oz flaked almonds

Heat 2 tablespoons of the oil in a pan, add 1 onion and fry until golden. Add the lamb and 175 g/6 oz of the yogurt; stir well, cover and simmer for 20 minutes.

Place the garlic, chopped ginger, chillies, coriander seeds, cumin, mint, chopped coriander and 2-3 tablespoons of the yogurt in a liquidizer or food processor and work to a paste.

Heat the remaining oil in a large pan, add the cardamoms, cloves and cinnamon and fry for 1 minute. Add the second onion, prepared paste and fry for 5 minutes, stirring constantly. Add the lamb and yogurt mixture and salt to taste. Bring to simmering point, cover and cook for 30 minutes. Add the almonds and cook for a further 15 minutes. Serve hot.

COOK'S TIP

If liked, serve the curry sprinkled with chopped fresh mint and garnished with fresh mint leaves. Serve with boiled rice and a selection of chutneys and relishes.

88 LAMB CURRY WITH COCONUT

Preparation time:
20 minutes

Cooking time:
about 1 hour 10 minutes

Serves 4

Calories:
690 per portion

YOU WILL NEED:
grated flesh of ½ fresh coconut
4 dried red chillies
1 teaspoon cumin seeds
1 tablespoon coriander seeds
1 tablespoon poppy seeds
1 teaspoon peppercorns
1 x 2.5 cm/½ inch piece root ginger, chopped
2 garlic cloves
1 teaspoon turmeric
2 tablespoons lemon juice
4 tablespoons oil
2 onions, chopped
4 curry leaves
750 g/1½ lb boned leg of lamb, cubed
1 x 227 g/8 oz can tomatoes
salt
2 tablespoons finely chopped coriander

Heat the coconut, chillies, cumin, coriander and poppy seeds in a dry frying pan for about 1 minute. Place in a food processor or liquidizer with the peppercorns, ginger, garlic, turmeric and lemon juice and blend to a paste.

Heat the oil in a pan, add the onions and fry until soft, then add the curry leaves and the prepared paste and fry for 5 minutes. Add the lamb and cook, stirring, for 5 minutes, then add the tomatoes with their juice and salt to taste. Bring to simmering point, cover and cook for about 1 hour until tender. Sprinkle with chopped coriander and serve.

COOK'S TIP

If fresh coconut is not available, blend the other spices and lemon juice as instructed, and add 50 g/2 oz creamed coconut to the onions with the spices.

89 STICK LAMB CURRY

Preparation time:
20 minutes

Cooking time:
50 minutes

Serves 4

Calories:
350 per portion

YOU WILL NEED:
450 g/1 lb boned leg of lamb, cubed
2 onions, layers separated and cut into
    squares
1 x 2.5 cm/1 inch piece root ginger, cut
    into thin slices
2 tablespoons oil
275 g/10 oz natural yogurt
1 teaspoon salt
FOR THE SPICE PASTE
1 onion, quartered
2 garlic cloves, peeled
1 tablespoon coriander seeds
1 x 2.5 cm/1 inch piece root ginger,
    chopped
½-1 teaspoon small dried red chillies
1 teaspoon turmeric

First make the spice paste, put all the ingredients in a blender
or food processor and work to a paste.

Thread the lamb, onion and ginger on to 8 wooden skewers. Heat the oil in a pan and fry the spice paste for 5 minutes,
adding a spoonful of water if necessary. Add the lamb skewers
and fry, turning occasionally for 3-4 minutes. Remove from
the pan and stir in the yogurt, then return the meat skewers
with the salt and 2-3 tablespoons water. Cover and simmer for
35 minutes or until the lamb is tender. Serve hot.

90 LAMB KORMA

Preparation time:
15 minutes

Cooking time:
about 1½ hours

Serves 4

Calories:
500 per portion

YOU WILL NEED:
5 tablespoons oil
6 cardamoms
6 cloves
6 peppercorns
1 x 2.5 cm/1 inch piece cinnamon stick
675 g/1½ lb boned leg of lamb, cubed
6 small onions, chopped
2 garlic cloves, chopped
1 x 5 cm/2 inch piece root ginger,
    chopped
2 tablespoons ground coriander
2 teaspoons ground cumin
1 teaspoon chilli powder
salt
150 g/5 oz natural yogurt
1 teaspoon garam masala

Heat 4 tablespoons of the oil in a pan, add the cardamoms,
cloves, peppercorns and cinnamon and fry for 1 minute. Add
the lamb, a few pieces at a time, and fry until browned on all
sides; transfer to a dish. Remove the whole spices and discard.

Add the remaining oil to the pan and fry the onions, garlic
and ginger for 5 minutes, then add the coriander, cumin, chilli
powder and salt to taste and cook for 5 minutes, stirring frequently. Gradually stir in the yogurt. Return the meat and any
juices and sufficient water to just cover the meat. Bring to simmering point, cover and cook for about 1 hour until tender.

Sprinkle on the garam masala and cook for 1 minute.
Serve at once.

▨ COOK'S TIP

*Make a pineapple raita to
serve with this: beat a little
salt and sugar into a bowl of
natural yogurt, stir in some
pineapple chunks and a
chopped green chilli.*

▨ COOK'S TIP

*Serve this mild curry with
rice, Poppadoms (recipe 188)
or Chapatis (recipe 186) and
a variety of chutneys (recipes
201-11). The dish is popular
in northern India.*

91 LAMB KARANGA

Preparation time:
25 minutes

Cooking time:
about 1½ hours

Serves 4

Calories:
730 per portion

YOU WILL NEED:
100 g/4 oz hard margarine
1 large onion, finely chopped
1 teaspoon cumin seeds, crushed
100 g/4 oz fresh, unroasted peanuts,
    finely ground
1 tablespoon ground coriander
1 teaspoon chilli powder
1 x 225 g/8 oz can tomatoes, chopped
    with the juice
1 teaspoon salt
750 g/1½ lb lamb, cubed
300 ml/½ pint water
150 ml/¼ pint soured cream

Melt the margarine in a large pan, add the onion and fry until lightly browned. Add the cumin seeds and peanuts and fry for 2-3 minutes, then add the coriander and chilli powder and fry for a few seconds. Stir in the tomatoes and salt. Fry for 4-5 minutes, then add the lamb and toss thoroughly in the mixture. Blend in the water, then cover and cook for about 1½ hours or until the meat is tender.

Serve on a bed of rice with the soured cream on top.

92 PORK VATANA

Preparation time:
25 minutes

Cooking time:
1-1¼ hours

Oven temperature:
180C, 350F, gas 4

Serves 4

Calories:
380 per portion

YOU WILL NEED:
450 g/1 lb pie pork or pork steak, cubed
1 large onion, chopped
2 garlic cloves, crushed
1 tablespoon ground coriander
1 tablespoon mustard powder
1 teaspoon ground cinnamon
1 teaspoon salt
1 teaspoon sugar
1 x 225 g/8 oz can tomatoes, chopped
    with the juice
50 ml/2 fl oz oil
1 x 425 g/15 oz can haricot beans,
    drained and liquid reserved
1 green pepper, seeded and sliced, to
    garnish

Place the meat in an ovenproof casserole dish. Mix together the onion, garlic, spices, salt, sugar, tomatoes, oil and liquid from the beans in a bowl. Pour this mixture evenly over the meat, cover and bake for 1 hour until the meat is tender.

Stir in the drained beans and cook for a further 15 minutes. Garnish with the green pepper slices and serve.

■ COOK'S TIP

To make soured cream, stir
1 teaspoon lemon juice into
150 ml/¼ pint fresh single
cream and leave to stand for
30 minutes before use.

■ COOK'S TIP

To use dried haricot beans
in this recipe, soak them
overnight and then cook
them in a pressure cooker for
about 10 minutes before
adding to the dish as above.

93 MASALA CHOPS

Preparation time:
10 minutes, plus 30
minutes standing time

Cooking time:
about 10-15 minutes

Serves 4

Calories:
570 per portion

YOU WILL NEED:
1 teaspoon ground cumin seeds
2 teaspoons ground coriander seeds
¼ teaspoon chilli powder
1 garlic clove, crushed
salt
lemon juice to mix
4 pork chops

Mix the cumin, coriander, chilli powder, garlic and salt to taste into a paste with lemon juice. Slash the pork chops on both sides. Rub the paste into the meat and leave for 30 minutes. Cook under a moderate grill for 5-6 minutes on each side. Serve hot.

94 PORK DHANSAK

Preparation time:
20-25 minutes, plus
soaking time

Cooking time:
1¼-1½ hours

Oven temperature:
180C, 350F, gas 4

Serves 4

Calories:
470 per portion

YOU WILL NEED:
450 g/1 lb pie pork or pork steak, cubed
100 g/4 oz dried red lentils, soaked for a
*   few hours and drained*
1 large onion, finely chopped
2 garlic cloves, crushed
85 ml/3 fl oz oil
2 tablespoons ground coriander
1 teaspoon garam masala
1 teaspoon ground cardamom
1 teaspoon ground white pepper
1 teaspoon salt
2 teaspoons sugar
1 x 400 g/14 oz can tomatoes, chopped
*   with the juice*
150 ml/¼ pint water

Trim off the excess fat from the meat and arrange in an oven-proof casserole dish. Mix all the remaining ingredients in a bowl and pour evenly over the meat. Cover and bake for 1¼-1½ hours, stirring once during the cooking time. Stir thoroughly before serving.

■ COOK'S TIP

Pork chops come from the loin or spare rib joints. If you buy them with rind on, cut through it with scissors or the chops will curl up as you cook them.

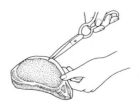

■ COOK'S TIP

White pepper has a sharper flavour than black pepper, and is used in some dishes whose delicate appearance would be spoilt by black specks of pepper. This dish *goes particularly well with Saffron Rice (recipe 176).*

95 PORK VINDALOO

Preparation time:
10 minutes, plus
overnight standing

Cooking time:
about 50 minutes

Serves 4

Calories:
370 per portion

YOU WILL NEED:
1-2 teaspoons chilli powder
1 teaspoon turmeric
2 teaspoons ground cumin
2 teaspoons ground mustard
2 tablespoons ground coriander
1 x 2.5 cm/1 inch piece root ginger,
   chopped
salt
150 ml/¼ pint vinegar
1 large onion, finely chopped
2 garlic cloves, crushed
675 g/1½ lb pork fillet, cubed
4 tablespoons oil

Mix the spices and salt to taste with the vinegar. Put the onion, garlic and pork in a bowl, pour over the vinegar mixture, cover and leave in the refrigerator overnight.

Heat the oil in a large pan, add the pork mixture, bring to simmering point, cover and cook for about 45 minutes or until the pork is tender.

96 CHILLI PORK AND PRAWNS

Preparation time:
15 minutes

Cooking time:
20 minutes

Serves 4

Calories:
180 per portion

YOU WILL NEED:
300 ml/½ pint thick coconut milk
225 g/8 oz raw peeled prawns, finely
   chopped
225 g/8 oz pork fillet, finely chopped
2 red chillies, finely chopped
1 teaspoon salt
1 teaspoon sugar
½ teaspoon freshly ground black pepper

Pour the coconut milk into a saucepan and bring to simmering point. Mix the prawns and pork together and stir into the coconut milk. Add the chillies, salt, sugar and pepper and simmer gently for 15-20 minutes. Transfer to a warmed serving dish and serve at once.

■ COOK'S TIP

A vindaloo dish, cooked with the addition of vinegar, tends to be hot, so it is a good idea to serve plenty of liquid with it. Remember that dry wines are not a good accompaniment to Indian food.

■ COOK'S TIP

This is a very hot curry on account of its use of fresh red chillies. For a less fiery flavour, discard the seeds and rinse the chillies under cold running water.

POULTRY DISHES

Chicken features quite prominently in Indian cookery, since poultry does not hold the taboos and dietary considerations required on religious grounds that red meat does. Chicken is usually skinned in Indian recipes in order to allow the flavours of the spices and other ingredients in which it is cooked to permeate the flesh.

97   CHICKEN IN APRICOTS

Preparation time:
30-35 minutes

Cooking time:
1½ hours

Oven temperature:
180C, 325F, gas 4

Serves 4

Calories:
370 per portion

YOU WILL NEED:
1 x 1.75 kg/4 lb chicken, skinned and
   jointed
50 ml/2 fl oz oil
2 large onions, finely chopped
2 garlic cloves, creamed
2 tablespoons ground coriander
1 teaspoon ground cardamom
1½ teaspoons chilli powder
1 teaspoon sugar
salt
1 x 400 g/14 oz can tomatoes, chopped
   with the juice
1 x 400 g/14 oz can apricots, drained
   and half the liquid reserved

Place the chicken joints in a large ovenproof casserole dish. Mix together the remaining ingredients in a bowl, adding salt to taste and half the fruit. Pour the mixture evenly over the chicken. Cover and bake for 1 hour.

Remove the casserole from the oven and gently spoon the sauce over the chicken pieces. Arrange the remaining fruit attractively on the chicken, then cover and cook for a further 30 minutes until the chicken is tender. Serve hot.

98   CHICKEN CURRY

Preparation time:
15 minutes, plus 4
hours marinating time

Cooking time:
about 35 minutes

Serves 4

Calories:
350 per portion

YOU WILL NEED:
2 garlic cloves, chopped
1 x 5 cm/2 inch piece root ginger, peeled
   and chopped
1 teaspoon turmeric
2 teaspoons cumin seeds, ground
1 teaspoon chilli powder
1 teaspoon pepper
3 tablespoons finely chopped fresh
   coriander leaves
450 g/1 lb natural yogurt
salt
1 kg/2 lb chicken pieces, skinned
4 tablespoons oil
2 onions, chopped

Put the garlic, ginger, turmeric, cumin, chilli powder, pepper, coriander, yogurt and salt to taste into a large bowl. Mix well, add the chicken and leave for 4 hours, turning the chicken occasionally.

Heat the oil in a pan, add the onions and fry until golden. Add the chicken and the marinade. Bring to simmering point, cover and cook for about 30 minutes, until the chicken is tender.

■ COOK'S TIP

Fresh apricots may be used in season in place of canned ones, but they must be sweetened. Place 450 g/1 lb fresh apricot halves in a pan with 300 ml/½ pint water and 2 tablespoons sugar. Poach gently until tender, and then remove the apricots and reduce the liquid to 150 ml/ ¼ pint.

■ COOK'S TIP

It is difficult to grind just a teaspoon or two of spices in a blender or food processor – this is best done in a pestle and mortar, coffee grinder or small herb mill.

99 CHICKEN IN COCONUT MILK

Preparation time:
30 minutes

Cooking time:
about 40 minutes

Serves 4

Calories:
290 per portion

YOU WILL NEED:
1 x 1.5 kg/3½ lb chicken, cut into 8
    pieces
900 ml/1½ pints coconut milk
1 x 5 cm/2 inch piece lengkuas (see
    Cook's Tip)
3 green chillies, seeded
8 stems coriander
4 citrus leaves (optional)
a few black peppercorns, crushed
1 teaspoon grated lime rind
salt
2 tablespoons fish sauce
1 tablespoon lime juice
fresh coriander leaves, to garnish

Skin the chicken and place in a pan. Skim off the coconut cream from the milk and reserve. Pour the remaining milk over the chicken. Finely chop the lengkuas, chillies and coriander stems. Add to the pan the citrus leaves, if using, the crushed peppercorns, lime rind and salt to taste. Bring to the boil, reduce the heat and simmer, uncovered, for 35-40 minutes or until the chicken is tender and half of the liquid has evaporated.

About 5 minutes before serving, pour in the reserved coconut cream and bring to the boil. Add the fish sauce and lime juice. Transfer to a warmed serving dish and sprinkle with coriander leaves to garnish.

■ COOK'S TIP

If only laos powder is available, rather than the fresh root, use 1 teaspoon laos powder for each 1 cm/ 1½ inch piece of lengkuas root specified in the recipe.

100 CHICKEN PILAU

Preparation time:
20 minutes, plus 30
minutes soaking time

Cooking time:
about 1¼ hours

Serves 6

Calories:
550 per portion

YOU WILL NEED:
350 g/12 oz Basmati rice
1 x 1.5 kg/3½ lb oven-ready chicken
5 tablespoons ghee or butter
1 x 5 cm/2 inch piece cinnamon stick
8 cloves
6 cardamom seeds
2 garlic cloves, crushed
½-1 teaspoon chilli powder
1 tablespoon fennel seeds
5 tablespoons natural yogurt
1 teaspoon powdered saffron
1½ teaspoons salt
about 600 ml/1 pint chicken stock
2 large onions, sliced

Wash the rice thoroughly and soak in cold fresh water for 30 minutes; drain. Skin the chicken and cut into pieces.

Melt the ghee or butter in a large flameproof casserole. Add the cinnamon, cloves and cardamom and fry for 30 seconds. Stir in the garlic, chilli powder and fennel and fry for 30 seconds. Add the chicken and fry, turning, for 5 minutes. Add the yogurt a spoonful at a time, stirring until absorbed before adding the next spoonful. Cover and simmer for 25 minutes.

Add the rice, saffron and salt. Fry, stirring, until the rice is well mixed. Add enough stock to cover the rice by 5 mm/¼ inch and bring to the boil. Reduce the heat to very low, cover tightly and cook for 20 minutes or until the rice is cooked.

Fry the onion in 4 tablespoons ghee until golden. Transfer the pilau to a dish and garnish with the onion.

■ COOK'S TIP

In a meat or poultry pilau the meat is cooked with the spices before the rice is added. The use of saffron is expensive, but it does enhance the flavour and appearance.

101 PINEAPPLE CHICKEN CURRY

Preparation time:
1 hour, including
soaking time

Cooking time:
45 minutes

Serves 4

Calories:
620 per portion

YOU WILL NEED:

2 onions, quartered
2 garlic cloves, peeled
1 x 3.5 cm/1 ½ inch piece root ginger,
    peeled and chopped
1 teaspoon turmeric
1 tablespoon ground coriander
1-2 teaspoons chilli powder
2 tablespoons paprika
1 teaspoon sugar
1 teaspoon salt
2 tablespoons oil
8 chicken thighs, skinned
300 ml/½ pint water
100 g/4 oz cashew nuts, soaked in
    boiling water for 1 hour
6 curry leaves
4 green chillies, slit
1 medium pineapple, cubed
juice of ½-1 lemon

Place the first 9 ingredients in a liquidizer or food processor and work until smooth.

Heat the oil, add the spice paste and fry for 10 minutes. Add the chicken pieces and fry for 5 minutes. Pour in the water and bring to simmering point. Add the drained nuts, curry leaves and chillies, cover and simmer for 25 minutes. Add the pineapple and lemon juice to taste and simmer for a further 10 minutes. Serve hot.

102 CHICKEN IN PEANUT SAUCE

Preparation time:
30 minutes

Cooking time:
1-1½ hours

Oven temperature:
180C, 325F, gas 4

Serves 4

Calories:
430 per portion

YOU WILL NEED:

1 x 1.75 kg/4 lb chicken, skinned and
    jointed
2 large onions, finely chopped
2 garlic cloves, crushed
100 g/4 oz peanut butter
1 x 400 g/14 oz can tomatoes, chopped
    with the juice
1 teaspoon ground cinnamon
1 tablespoon ground cumin
1 teaspoon chilli powder
2 teaspoons paprika
2 teaspoons brown sugar
1 teaspoon salt
2 tablespoons lemon juice
1-2 sprigs fresh coriander leaves,
    to garnish

Using a sharp knife, make a few slanting cuts on the fleshy part of the chicken joints, then place them in an ovenproof casserole dish.

Mix together the remaining ingredients in a bowl and pour the sauce evenly over the chicken. Cover and bake for about 1-1½ hours or until the chicken is tender. Stir the sauce and baste the chicken joints once during the cooking time. Garnish with the coriander sprigs and serve.

◼ COOK'S TIP

Fruits such as pineapple, bananas, mangoes and grapes provide an excellent foil for curries. Serve them as sauces, relishes or simply sliced in bowls.

◼ COOK'S TIP

This dish is excellent served with Plain Boiled Rice (recipe 182) to bring out the nutty flavour of the sauce. Use crunchy peanut butter rather than the smooth variety.

103 SPICY CHICKEN

Preparation time:
35 minutes, including marinating time

Cooking time:
45 minutes

Serves 4

Calories:
400 per portion

YOU WILL NEED:
8 chicken pieces, skinned
juice of 1 lemon
4 tablespoons desiccated coconut,
    soaked in 4 tablespoons hot water
2-4 red chillies, chopped
4 small onions, quartered
2 garlic cloves, peeled
4 Brazil nuts, shelled
1 x 1 cm/½ inch piece root ginger,
    peeled
1 teaspoon grated lemon rind
1 teaspoon shrimp paste
1 teaspoon sugar
1 teaspoon salt
3 tablespoons oil
300 ml/½ pint water

Rub the chicken pieces with the lemon juice and leave to stand for 20 minutes.

Put all the remaining ingredients except the oil and water in a liquidizer or food processor and work to a smooth paste. Heat the oil in a large pan and fry the paste, stirring, for 5 minutes.

Add the chicken and fry for 5 minutes. Stir in the water and cook, uncovered, for 30 minutes or until the chicken is tender and the sauce is thick. Serve hot.

▇ COOK'S TIP

You can make an attractive garnish for this dish by shaving a few nuts lengthways with a potato peeler and grilling them until golden brown and curled.

104 CHICKEN KORMA

Preparation time:
15 minutes, plus overnight chilling time

Cooking time:
1½-1¾ hours

Serves 4

Calories:
520 per portion

YOU WILL NEED:
175 g/6 oz natural yogurt
2 teaspoons turmeric
3 garlic cloves, sliced
1 x 1.5 kg/3 lb roasting chicken
100 g/4 oz ghee
1 large onion, sliced
1 teaspoon ground ginger
1 x 5 cm/2 inch piece cinnamon stick
5 cloves
5 cardamoms
1 tablespoon crushed coriander seeds
1 teaspoon ground cumin
½ teaspoon chilli powder
1 teaspoon salt
1½ tablespoons desiccated coconut
2 teaspoons roasted almonds

Place the yogurt, turmeric and 1 garlic clove in a food processor or liquidizer and purée to mix evenly. Place the chicken in a dish and pour over the yogurt mixture. Cover and place in the refrigerator to chill overnight.

Melt the ghee in a large saucepan, add the onion and remaining garlic and fry gently for 4-5 minutes until soft. Add the spices and salt and fry for a further 3 minutes, stirring constantly.

Add the chicken with the yogurt marinade and coconut and turn the chicken in the marinade to coat it well. Cover and simmer for 1¼-1½ hours until the chicken is tender. Transfer to a warmed serving dish and scatter with the almonds.

▇ COOK'S TIP

This dish may be cooked more quickly if the chicken is cut into pieces before chilling it overnight in the marinade. Simmering time would be about 45 minutes.

105 MURGH MUSSALAM

Preparation time:
20 minutes, plus
1 hour standing time

Cooking time:
about 1¾ hours

Serves 4

Calories:
550 per portion

YOU WILL NEED:
2 onions
2 garlic cloves
1 x 5 cm/2 inch piece root ginger, peeled
1 teaspoon poppy seeds
8 peppercorns
300 ml/½ pint natural yogurt
1 teaspoon garam masala
1 x 1.5 kg/3 lb oven-ready chicken
100 g/4 oz long-grain rice, soaked in
  cold water for 1 hour
3 tablespoons ghee
½ teaspoon chilli powder
50 g/2 oz sultanas
50 g/2 oz slivered almonds
350 ml/12 fl oz water

Work the onions, garlic, ginger, poppy seeds, peppercorns and half the yogurt to a paste in a food processor. Stir in the garam masala and add salt to taste. Prick the chicken all over and rub in the blended mixture. Leave for 1 hour. Drain the rice.

Heat 1 tablespoon of the ghee in a pan, add the rice and stir-fry for 3 minutes. Add the chilli powder, sultanas, almonds and salt. Pour in half the water, cover and simmer for about 10 minutes, until the rice is almost tender. Stuff the chicken with the cooled rice; sew up both ends. Heat the remaining ghee in a pan and add the chicken, on its side. Pour in any marinade and the remaining water. Simmer, covered, for 1 hour. Add the remaining yogurt, a spoonful at a time, stirring until it is all absorbed. Cook for a further 15 minutes.

▪ COOK'S TIP

Never forget to remove the giblets before cooking a whole chicken. If using a frozen bird for this recipe, ensure it is completely defrosted before cooking.

Leave it to defrost in its wrappings in the refrigerator for about 24 hours.

106 BUTTER CHICKEN

Preparation time:
30 minutes, plus 4-5
hours marinating time

Cooking time:
50-60 minutes

Oven temperature:
220C, 425F, gas 7

Serves 8

Calories:
370 per portion

YOU WILL NEED:
1 x 1.5 kg/3½ lb chicken, cut into
  8 pieces
salt
1 tablespoon lemon juice
1 green chilli, chopped
7 g/¼ oz root ginger, peeled
3 small garlic cloves, peeled
150 ml/¼ pint natural yogurt
2 teaspoons paprika
¼ teaspoon chilli powder
orange food colouring (optional)
a little melted butter
175 g/6 oz unsalted butter
150 ml/¼ pint soured cream

Make sharp slits through the skin of the chicken, rub with salt and sprinkle with lemon juice. Purée the chilli with the ginger and garlic. Mix with the yogurt, paprika, chilli powder and orange colouring if liked. Mix with the chicken and marinate for 4-5 hours.

Remove the chicken portions and place on a baking tray and bake for 45-50 minutes, brushing with a little butter occasionally.

Melt the butter in a pan, add the marinade and soured cream and heat, without boiling, for 5-6 minutes. Pour over the chicken to serve.

▪ COOK'S TIP

50 g/2 oz finely chopped cashew nuts or almonds can be added to the simmering sauce if liked. Serve as a main course with Naan bread (see recipe 192).

107 SHREDDED CHICKEN FRY

Preparation time:
about 50 minutes,
plus 1 hour
marinating time

Cooking time:
25-30 minutes

Serves 4-6

Calories:
300-200 per portion

YOU WILL NEED:
*2 green chillies, seeded and roughly
    chopped*
3 garlic cloves
50 g/2 oz fresh root ginger, peeled
1 large onion, roughly chopped
1 tablespoon vinegar
*4 chicken breasts, skinned, boned and
    shredded*
3 teaspoons ground cumin
2 teaspoons freshly ground black pepper
salt
40 g/1½ oz ghee or 3 tablespoons oil
2 green peppers, seeded and sliced
juice of 1 lemon

Grind the chillies, garlic, ginger, onion and vinegar to a paste. Place the shredded chicken and the paste in a large bowl, mix thoroughly, then cover and set aside for 1 hour to marinate.

Add the cumin, pepper and salt to the marinated mixture and mix well. Heat the ghee or oil in a large pan, add the chicken, cover and fry over a gentle heat for 15-20 minutes.

Add the green pepper, leave the pan uncovered and fry for a further 10 minutes until the mixture is fairly dry and the chicken is cooked. Sprinkle with the lemon juice before serving.

108 CHICKEN MOLEE

Preparation time:
15 minutes

Cooking time:
about 40 minutes

Serves 4

Calories:
350 per portion

YOU WILL NEED:
3 tablespoons oil
*4 chicken breasts, skinned, boned and
    diced*
6 cardamoms
6 cloves
1 x 5 cm/2 inch piece cinnamon stick
1 large onion, sliced
2 garlic cloves, peeled
*1 x 4 cm/1½ inch piece root ginger,
    peeled and chopped*
3 green chillies, seeded
juice of 1 lemon
1 teaspoon turmeric
50 g/2 oz creamed coconut
150 ml/¼ pint hot water
salt

Heat the oil in a pan, add the chicken and fry quickly on all sides to brown. Remove with a slotted spoon.

Add the cardamoms, cloves and cinnamon and fry for 1 minute. Add the onion and fry until soft.

Purée the garlic, ginger, chillies and lemon juice in a liquidizer or food processor. Add to the pan with the turmeric and cook for 5 minutes.

Melt the coconut in the hot water and add to the pan with salt to taste. Simmer for 2 minutes, then add the chicken pieces and any juices. Simmer for 15-20 minutes, until tender.

COOK'S TIP

Serve this chicken recipe as a light meal with one of the Indian breads (recipes 188-92), or as a side dish to accompany a pulse or vegetable curry such as Lentil *Coconut Curry (recipe 163) or Vegetable Curry (recipe 145).*

COOK'S TIP

Creamed coconut, sold as a block, is used in many Oriental dishes. It can be used in its concentrated form in a dish, or made up to make coconut milk.

109 KASHMIRI CHICKEN

Preparation time:
10 minutes

Cooking time:
about 40 minutes

Serves 6

Calories:
320 per portion

YOU WILL NEED:
100 g/4 oz butter
3 large onions, finely sliced
10 peppercorns
10 cardamoms
1 x 5 cm/2 inch piece cinnamon stick
1 x 5 cm/2 inch piece root ginger,
 chopped
2 cloves garlic, finely chopped
1 teaspoon chilli powder
2 teaspoons paprika
salt
1.5 kg/3 lb chicken pieces, skinned
250 ml/8 fl oz natural yogurt
FOR THE GARNISH
lime wedges
sprigs of parsley

Melt the butter in a deep, lidded frying pan or wok. Add the onions, peppercorns, cardamoms and cinnamon and fry until the onions are golden. Add the ginger, garlic, chilli powder, paprika and salt to taste and fry for 2 minutes, stirring occasionally.

Add the chicken pieces and fry until browned. Gradually add the yogurt, stirring constantly. Cover and cook for about 30 minutes. Serve hot, garnished with lime wedges and sprigs of parsley if liked.

110 CURRIED CHICKEN

Preparation time:
10 minutes

Cooking time:
8 minutes

Serves 4

Calories:
200 per portion

YOU WILL NEED:
2 tablespoons oil
½ teaspoon cumin seeds
½ teaspoon ground cinnamon
seeds from 2 cardamoms, crushed
pepper
2 onions, chopped
1 heaped teaspoon chopped root ginger
2 garlic cloves, crushed
3-4 chicken breasts, skinned and cut
 into slivers
1 x 400 g/14 oz can tomatoes
1 tablespoon soy sauce
1-2 teaspoons sugar
½ teaspoon garam masala

Heat the oil and fry the cumin seeds, cinnamon and cardamom seeds for 1 minute. Add the pepper, onions, ginger and garlic and fry for 2 minutes. Add the chicken pieces and stir-fry for about 5 minutes, until lightly coloured. Add the tomatoes, with their juice, soy sauce and sugar to taste. Bring to the boil, lower the heat and stir in the garam masala. Serve at once.

■ COOK'S TIP

Ring the changes by garnishing with flat-leaved (or Italian) parsley instead of the usual curly-leaved variety. Parsley fried in deep fat makes an unusual garnish.

■ COOK'S TIP

Serve this curry with poppadoms, wholewheat chapatis or rice. A fruit chutney and side dishes of cucumber and grated carrot will complete the course.

111 DRY CHICKEN CURRY

Preparation time:
15 minutes

Cooking time:
about 1 hour 10 minutes

Serves 4

Calories:
290 per portion

YOU WILL NEED:
50 g/2 oz butter
1 large onion, chopped
1 garlic clove, crushed
2 teaspoons curry powder
2 teaspoons salt
1 teaspoon chilli powder
1 x 1.25 kg/2 ½ lb chicken, jointed
150 ml/¼ pint water
450 g/1 lb tomatoes, peeled and quartered
2 tablespoons natural yogurt

Melt the butter in a large pan, add the onion and garlic and fry gently until golden. Add the curry powder, salt, chilli powder and chicken. Fry, stirring occasionally, until the chicken joints are brown all over. Add the water, cover the pan and simmer gently for 45 minutes. Add the tomatoes and yogurt and simmer for a further 5 minutes.

112 YOGURT CHICKEN

Preparation time:
10 minutes, plus 8 hours marinating time

Cooking time:
about 1¼-1½ hours

Oven temperatures:
200C, 400F, gas 6 then 180C, 350F, gas 4

Serves 4

Calories:
280 per portion

YOU WILL NEED:
1 x 1.5 kg/3 ½ lb chicken, skinned
2 tablespoons lemon juice
1 teaspoon salt
250 ml/8 fl oz natural yogurt
½ bunch fresh coriander leaves, finely chopped
1 x 5 cm/2 inch piece root ginger, peeled and chopped
4 garlic cloves, finely chopped
2 small green chillies, seeded and finely chopped
FOR THE GARNISH (OPTIONAL)
cucumber slices
lemon slices

Prick the chicken all over and rub with the lemon juice and salt. Cover and leave to stand for 30 minutes.

Mix the yogurt with the coriander, ginger, garlic and chillies, rub over the chicken and leave to stand for 7-8 hours.

Place in a roasting tin and cook at the higher temperature for 30 minutes. Reduce the temperature and cook for a further 45 minutes or until cooked. Remove the chicken from the juices and keep warm. Skim off the fat from the juices, bring to the boil and cook for 2-3 minutes until thickened. Pour over the chicken and garnish with cucumber and lemon slices if liked.

■ COOK'S TIP

Serve this with Saffron Rice (recipe 176), a bowl of salted peanuts and a dish of raw onion rings.

■ COOK'S TIP

To test whether a chicken is cooked, push a skewer into the meaty part. If any red or pink juices flow out, the chicken is not yet cooked.

113 CHICKEN AND DHAL CURRY

Preparation time:
15 minutes, plus
1 hour soaking time

Cooking time:
about 2 hours

Serves 4

Calories:
470 per portion

YOU WILL NEED:
225 g/8 oz masoor dhal
600 ml/1 pint water
salt
3 tablespoons oil
2 onions, minced
2 garlic cloves, minced
1 x 2.5 cm/1 inch piece root ginger,
    peeled and minced
1 tablespoon ground coriander seeds
1 teaspoon ground cumin seeds
½ teaspoon turmeric
½ teaspoon ground cloves
2 teaspoons chilli powder
750 g/1½ lb chicken thighs

Wash the dhal, soak in fresh cold water for 1 hour, then drain and boil in the water with 1 teaspoon salt added, for about 1 hour until soft. Drain and set aside.

Heat the oil in a saucepan, add the onion, garlic and ginger and fry for about 5 minutes. Add the spices and salt to taste and fry gently for 10 minutes; if the mixture becomes too dry, add 2 tablespoons water. Add the chicken and fry until golden all over. Add the cooked dhal, cover and simmer for about 30 minutes until the chicken is tender.

114 GREEN CHICKEN CURRY

Preparation time:
10 minutes

Cooking time:
45 minutes

Serves 4

Calories:
540 per portion

YOU WILL NEED:
1 x 5 cm/2 inch piece root ginger, peeled
    and chopped
40 g/1½ oz fresh coriander leaves,
    chopped
2-4 green chillies, chopped
4 garlic cloves
2 onions, quartered
1 tablespoon plain flour
salt
1 teaspoon chilli powder
8 chicken thighs, skinned
3 tablespoons oil
300 ml/½ pint water
50 g/2 oz creamed coconut
juice of 1 lemon
lemon twists, to garnish

Place the ginger, coriander, chillies, garlic and onions in a liquidizer or food processor and purée.

Mix the flour, 1 teaspoon salt and the chilli powder together and use to coat the chicken. Heat the oil, add the chicken and fry until golden. Remove and set aside.

Add the spice paste to the pan and fry, stirring, for 5 minutes. Stir in the water and salt to taste, then return the chicken to the pan. Cover and simmer for 25 minutes.

Stir in the coconut, then add the lemon juice; cover and simmer for 10 minutes. Serve at once garnished with lemon twists.

■ COOK'S TIP

Masoor dhal are Egyptian lentils: the orange ones widely available in most supermarkets and shops. Together with dried beans and peas, they are one of the *most popular pulses used in Indian cookery.*

■ COOK'S TIP

This green chicken curry gets its colour and flavour from coriander leaves. It goes well with rice and peas, or with Paratha (see recipe 190) or crusty French bread.

115 RICE COOKED WITH CHICKEN

Preparation time:
30 minutes

Cooking time:
about 3-3¼ hours

Serves 6

Calories:
880 per portion

YOU WILL NEED:
4 small onions, halved
2 bay leaves
1 litre/1¾ pints water
1 x 1.75 kg/4 lb boiling chicken
½ teaspoon saffron threads
675 g/1½ lb Basmati rice
100 g/4 oz ghee
5 garlic cloves, sliced
10 cloves
10 cardamoms
2 x 7.5 cm/3 inch cinnamon sticks
50 g/2 oz blanched almonds
100 g/4 oz sultanas
FOR THE GARNISH
hard-boiled egg quarters
fried onion rings

Place the onion halves, bay leaves and water in a pan and bring to the boil. Add the chicken, cover and simmer for 1½-2 hours until tender. Remove the flesh from the chicken and cut into pieces; reserve the cooking liquid and onions. Put the saffron in a cup and pour over a little boiling water; leave for 20 minutes. Wash the rice well.

Heat the ghee in a pan, add the reserved onions, garlic, cloves, cardamoms and cinnamon and fry for 5 minutes. Add the rice and enough cooking liquid to cover the rice, then the strained saffron water. Cook, uncovered, for 10-15 minutes, then cover to cook until tender. Mix with the chicken, almonds and sultanas. Garnish and serve.

116 TOMATO CHICKEN CURRY

Preparation time:
30 minutes

Cooking time:
1 hour-1 hour 10 minutes

Serves 8

Calories:
160 per portion

YOU WILL NEED:
40 g/1½ oz ghee or 3 tablespoons oil
1 onion, peeled and sliced
1 x 2.5 cm/1 inch piece cinnamon stick
4 small green cardamoms
2 green chillies, halved and seeded
50 g/2 oz root ginger, peeled and finely sliced
6-7 garlic cloves, sliced
1 x 1½ kg/3-3½ lb chicken, cut into 8 pieces
2 teaspoons ground cumin
3-4 sprigs fresh coriander leaves, chopped
1 x 400 g/14 oz can tomatoes
salt

Heat the ghee or oil in a very large saucepan and fry the onion until lightly browned. Add the cinnamon, cardamoms and chillies and fry for 1 minute, then add the sliced ginger and garlic. Fry for 30 seconds, add the chicken portions and fry for a further 10-15 minutes.

Add the cumin and coriander leaves and fry for 1-2 minutes, then stir in the tomatoes and salt to taste. Cover and cook over a gentle heat for 30-35 minutes until the chicken is tender.

▮ COOK'S TIP

To prevent black rings forming around the yolks of hard-boiled eggs, after cooking drain and leave in a saucepan under a running cold tap for about 2 minutes.

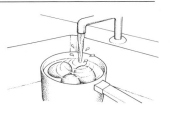

▮ COOK'S TIP

Melamine chopping boards do not absorb the smells of such foods as onions and garlic as wooden chopping boards do, but remember to keep knives well sharpened – *they blunt more quickly on melamine.*

117 WHITE CHICKEN CURRY

Preparation time:
15 minutes

Cooking time:
about 35 minutes

Serves 4

Calories:
350 per portion

YOU WILL NEED:
3 tablespoons vegetable oil
2 onions, finely sliced
8 long green chillies, finely cut
    lengthways
1 x 2.5 cm/1 inch piece fresh root
    ginger, finely sliced
1 teaspoon salt
75 g/3 oz creamed coconut, melted in
    450 ml/¾ pint water
4 chicken thighs and 4 chicken legs,
    skinned
juice of 2 small limes

Heat the oil in a saucepan, add the onions and fry gently for 3 minutes (do not let the onions colour). Add the chillies, ginger and salt. Stir well, then pour in the coconut mixture.

Add the chicken and simmer gently, uncovered, for 30 minutes or so until cooked through. Stir occasionally and if there is any hint of the sauce catching, add a little water.

When ready, remove from the heat, stir in the lime juice and serve at once.

118 CHILLI CHICKEN

Preparation time:
15 minutes

Cooking time:
about 10 minutes

Serves 4

Calories:
360 per portion

YOU WILL NEED:
675 g/1 ½ lb boneless chicken breasts,
    cubed
1 teaspoon sugar
3-6 red chillies
4 almonds
1 stem lemon grass, sliced
1 teaspoon fenugreek
1 x 2.5 cm/1 inch piece root ginger,
    peeled
6 small red onions or shallots, peeled
    and sliced
4 garlic cloves, crushed
4 tablespoons oil
150 ml/¼ pint water
salt
shredded spring onion, to garnish

Sprinkle the chicken with the sugar. Purée the chillies with the nuts, lemon grass, fenugreek and half the ginger. Purée the remaining ginger with the onions and garlic.

Heat the oil and fry the spice mixture for 1-2 minutes. Add the onion mixture and fry for 1-2 minutes. Add the chicken pieces and stir to coat. Add the water and salt to taste. Cover and cook gently for 5 minutes.

Transfer to a serving dish and sprinkle with the shredded spring onion to serve.

■ COOK'S TIP

Serve this with Pilau Rice (recipe 183), an Indian bread (recipes 188-92) and Raita or Zalata (recipes 193 or 197).

■ COOK'S TIP

Fresh red hot chillies are a major and important ingredient in this recipe both for their flavour and colour. They may be seeded if liked before use.

119 CHICKEN VINDALOO

Preparation time:
20 minutes

Cooking time:
about 1 hour

Serves 4

Calories:
800 per portion

YOU WILL NEED:
1 x 1.5 kg/3 ½ lb chicken
2 large onions, chopped
225 g/8 oz ghee
2 green chillies
25 g/1 oz root ginger, chopped
3 garlic cloves, chopped
1 ½ teaspoons turmeric
1 teaspoon ground coriander
1 teaspoon garam masala
2 tablespoons vinegar
2 curry leaves (optional)
300 ml/½ pint water
1 teaspoon salt
50 g/2 oz desiccated coconut
chopped fresh coriander, to garnish

Skin and joint the chicken. Fry the onions in the ghee with the ground chillies until golden. Add the ginger, garlic, turmeric, coriander and garam masala. Fry for a further 3 minutes.

Add the vinegar, curry leaves, if used, water and chicken. Cover and simmer for 30 minutes. Test to check that the chicken is cooked; it is cooked when the juices run clear after piercing the thickest part of the thigh with a knife or skewer. Remove the lid and boil rapidly until the liquid evaporates.

Add the salt and coconut and simmer for 15 minutes. Serve sprinkled with chopped coriander.

120 TANDOORI CHICKEN

Preparation time:
20 minutes, plus overnight marinating time

Cooking time:
1 hour

Oven temperature:
200C, 400F, gas 6

Serves 4

Calories:
370 per portion

YOU WILL NEED:
½-1 teaspoon chilli powder
1 teaspoon pepper
1 teaspoon salt
2 tablespoons lemon juice
1 x 1.5 kg/3 ½ lb chicken, skinned
50 g/2 oz butter, melted
FOR THE PASTE
4 tablespoons natural yogurt
3 garlic cloves
1 x 5 cm/2 inch piece root ginger, peeled
2 small dried red chillies
1 tablespoon coriander seeds
2 teaspoons cumin seeds

Mix the chilli powder, pepper, salt and lemon juice together. Slash the chicken all over and rub the mixture into the cuts; leave to stand for 1 hour.

Put all the paste ingredients in a liquidizer or food processor and work to a paste. Spread over the chicken, cover and chill overnight then bring to room temperature.

Place the chicken on a rack in a roasting pan and pour over half of the butter. Bake for 1 hour or until tender, pouring over the remaining butter after ½ hour's cooking. Serve either hot or cold.

■ COOK'S TIP

You need a strong vinegar to withstand the other flavours in this recipe: use malt or cider vinegar. The flavour of wine and rice vinegars is too subtle for such a fiery dish.

■ COOK'S TIP

The tandoor is a beehive-shaped clay oven heated by charcoal. The temperatures reached are very high, so tandoori recipes always involve quick cooking. Meat *and poultry is usually marinated before cooking to impart flavour.*

VEGETABLE & PULSE DISHES

Since much of the Indian population is vegetarian, vegetable and pulse dishes play a very important role in the cuisine of the country.

121 DHAI BHINDI

Preparation time:
15 minutes

Cooking time:
15-20 minutes

Serves 4

Calories:
70 per portion

YOU WILL NEED:
225 g/8 oz okra
2 tablespoons oil
1 x 2.5 cm/1 inch piece root ginger, peeled and chopped
1 teaspoon turmeric
salt
2-3 tablespoons water
300 ml/½ pint natural yogurt
½ teaspoon chilli powder
2 tablespoons grated fresh coconut
1 tablespoon finely chopped fresh coriander leaves

Cut the tops off the okra and halve lengthways. Heat the oil in a pan, add the okra and fry for 5 minutes. Add the ginger, turmeric and salt to taste, stir well. Add the water, cover and cook for 10 minutes until the okra is tender.

Mix the remaining ingredients together. Add to the pan, stir well and serve.

122 CAULIFLOWER RANGEEN

Preparation time:
30 minutes

Cooking time:
35-45 minutes

Serves 4

Calories:
170 per portion

YOU WILL NEED:
50 ml/2 fl oz oil
1 tablespoon cumin seeds
1 medium onion, sliced
450 g/1 lb cauliflower, broken into florets
100 g/4 oz fresh or frozen peas
100 g/4 oz carrots, cut into strips about 5 cm/2 inches long
1 tablespoon ground coriander
1 teaspoon turmeric
1 teaspoon chilli powder
salt
5-6 sprigs fresh coriander leaves, chopped, to garnish

Heat the oil in a large pan, add the cumin seeds and fry until they crackle. Add the onion and fry quickly until lightly browned. Reduce the heat and carefully add the prepared vegetables and the remaining ingredients except the fresh coriander. Stir well, cover and cook the vegetables in their own juices over a low heat for 30-40 minutes until they are tender and most of the liquid has evaporated.

A few minutes before serving, sprinkle the fresh coriander over the vegetables. Serve hot.

COOK'S TIP

To crack open a coconut without waste, put it in a roasting tin and place in the oven at 150C, 300F, gas 2 for about 25 minutes. It should crack by itself while cooking. Leave to cool, then grate the flesh as required.

COOK'S TIP

If your cooking oil goes cloudy, stand the bottle in a bowl of hot water until it is clear again. Keep oils in a kitchen cupboard, not the refrigerator.

123 STUFFED AUBERGINES

Preparation time:
15 minutes

Cooking time:
15-20 minutes

Serves 4

Calories:
160 per portion

YOU WILL NEED:
8 small aubergines
2 tablespoons ground coriander
1 tablespoon ground cumin
1 teaspoon garam masala
2 teaspoons mango powder
salt
chilli powder
2-3 tablespoons oil
2 small onions, quartered

Carefully slit the aubergines lengthways into 4 sections, held together at the stalk end. Mix all the ground spices and mango powder with salt and chilli powder to taste and carefully stuff some of the mixture into each of the aubergines, pressing the sections back together.

Heat the oil in a large frying pan, add the aubergines and onion quarters and fry over a gentle heat, turning carefully once or twice, until tender. Serve hot or cold.

124 KOBI GAAJER

Preparation time:
20-25 minutes

Cooking time:
35-45 minutes

Serves 4

Calories:
250 per portion

YOU WILL NEED:
85 ml/3 fl oz oil
1 tablespoon cumin seeds
450 g/1 lb white cabbage, finely shredded
225 g/8 oz carrots, diced
1 tablespoon ground coriander
1 teaspoon chilli powder
2 teaspoons salt
1 x 225 g/8 oz can tomatoes, chopped with the juice
5-6 sprigs fresh coriander leaves, chopped, to garnish

Heat the oil in a large pan, add the cumin seeds and fry until they crackle. Carefully add the cabbage and carrots. Reduce the heat and add the ground coriander, chilli powder and salt and mix well. Stir in the tomatoes. Cover and cook over a low heat for about 30-45 minutes, stirring frequently, until almost dry. Sprinkle with the fresh coriander and serve.

■ COOK'S TIP

Cover the pan if the oil starts to splutter during cooking – but remember to keep the heat low to ensure a good tender result.

■ COOK'S TIP

Firm white cabbage is good for salads and coleslaws, as well as in this dry curry with carrots. This dish is good served with Lamb Curry in the Oven (recipe 82).

125 KABLI CHANNA

Preparation time:
20 minutes, plus
overnight soaking

Cooking time:
about 1¾ hours

Serves 4

Calories:
270 per portion

YOU WILL NEED:

225 g/8 oz chick peas or Bengal gram
750 ml/1¼ pints water
1 teaspoon salt
2 tablespoons oil or concentrated butter
1 onion, chopped
1 x 2.5 cm/1 inch piece cinnamon stick
4 cloves
2 garlic cloves, crushed
1 x 2.5 cm/1 inch piece root ginger,
     peeled and chopped
2 green chillies, finely chopped
2 teaspoons ground coriander
150 g/5 oz tomatoes, chopped
1 teaspoon garam masala
1 tablespoon chopped fresh coriander
     leaves

Wash the chick peas or gram and soak in the water overnight. Add the salt and simmer until tender. Drain, reserving the water, and set aside.

Heat the oil or butter in a pan, add the onion and fry until golden. Add the cinnamon and cloves and fry for a few seconds, then add the garlic, ginger, chillies and ground coriander and fry for 5 minutes. Add the tomatoes and fry until most of the liquid has evaporated.

Add the cooked gram and cook gently for 5 minutes, then add the reserved water and simmer for 20-25 minutes. Add the garam masala and stir well. Sprinkle with the chopped coriander and serve at once.

■ COOK'S TIP

Kabli Channa or Bengal gram (whole peas) can be bought in most supermarkets and Indian shops, and may be used in this recipe instead of the chick peas. Use canned chick peas, drained, for convenience if you prefer.

126 PALAK ALOO

Preparation time:
10 minutes

Cooking time:
15-20 minutes

Serves 4

Calories:
180 per portion (300
with additional ghee)

YOU WILL NEED:

40 g/1½ oz ghee or butter
225 g/8 oz potatoes, peeled and cut into
     chunks
2 teaspoons garlic paste
2 teaspoons ginger paste
1 green chilli, halved and seeded
450 g/1 lb spinach, roughly chopped
1 tablespoon chopped fresh coriander
     leaves
salt
50 g/2 oz melted butter or ghee, for
     serving (optional)

Heat the ghee or butter in a pan and fry the potatoes for 4-5 minutes. Add the garlic and ginger pastes and the chilli. Fry for 1-2 minutes.

Stir in the spinach, coriander and salt to taste. Add a little water and continue frying for 10-15 minutes until the potatoes are tender and the spinach is dry.

Serve hot, with melted butter or ghee poured over the top if liked.

■ COOK'S TIP

If liked, frozen chopped spinach can be used in this recipe. You will need 225 g/ 8 oz which must be defrosted and squeezed dry in a fine sieve before use.

127 PEAS WITH INDIAN CHEESE CURRY

Preparation time:
5 minutes

Cooking time:
17 minutes

Serves 4

Calories:
630 per portion

YOU WILL NEED:
100 g/4 oz ghee
450 g/2 lb panir (Indian curd cheese),
   cubed
1 onion, sliced
1 teaspoon ground ginger
½ teaspoon ground cumin
½ teaspoon chilli powder
½ teaspoon salt
450 g/1 lb frozen peas
2 tomatoes, chopped

Melt the ghee in a medium frying pan, add the cheese and fry until browned on all sides. Remove, drain on absorbent kitchen paper and set aside.

Add the onion to the frying pan and fry gently for 4-5 minutes until soft. Add the ginger, cumin, chilli powder and salt and fry for a further 3 minutes, stirring constantly. Add the peas and tomatoes and stir gently until the peas are coated with the spice mixture. Stir in the cheese and heat through, taking care not to break up the cubes of cheese. Serve at once.

128 DRY OKRA CURRY

Preparation time:
15 minutes

Cooking time:
20-30 minutes

Serves 4-6

Calories:
180-120 per portion

YOU WILL NEED:
450 g/1 lb okra
40 g/1½ oz ghee or 3 tablespoons oil
1 medium onion, chopped
225 g/8 oz potatoes, cubed
about 1 teaspoon chilli powder
1½ teaspoons ground coriander
½ teaspoon turmeric
salt

Wash, dry, top and tail the okra, then chop it into 1 cm/½ inch lengths. As okra has a gluey sap it should always be washed, dried and then cut. Heat the ghee or oil in a pan, add the onion and fry until soft. Add the potatoes and fry for a further 3-5 minutes.

Stir in the okra, chilli powder, coriander, turmeric and salt to taste. Cover and fry gently for 10-12 minutes until the potatoes are tender. If the mixture becomes too dry, add 1 teaspoon oil or ghee, or a little water. Serve hot.

▩ COOK'S TIP

Cheese is not widely used in Indian cookery, but panir – a simple curd cheese – is a popular part of the country's cuisine. To make your own, see Cook's Tip, recipe 230.

▩ COOK'S TIP

Okra, also known as 'ladies fingers' and 'gumbo', should be firm, fresh and green. Avoid large, limp and brown ones. It goes well with onions, tomatoes and peppers.

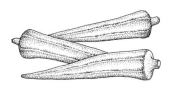

129 DHAL SAG

Preparation time:
10 minutes

Cooking time:
1 hour 10 minutes

Serves 4

Calories:
370 per portion

YOU WILL NEED:
225 g/8 oz moong dhal lentils, washed
   and drained
600 ml/1 pint water
3 onions, 1 sliced and 2 finely chopped
1 teaspoon chilli powder
½ teaspoon turmeric
salt
3 tablespoons oil
1 garlic clove, finely chopped
2 green chillies, finely chopped
2 teaspoons finely grated root ginger
1 teaspoon fennel seeds
1 kg/2 lb spinach, washed and chopped

Put the dhal, water, sliced onion, chilli powder, turmeric and 1 teaspoon salt in a pan and bring to the boil, then partially cover the pan and simmer for 1 hour.

In another pan, heat the oil, add the chopped onions and garlic and fry until soft and golden. Stir in the chillies, ginger and fennel seeds and fry for 1 minute. Add the spinach and cook, stirring, for 10 minutes. Stir in the dhal and continue to cook for 5-10 minutes. Add more salt if necessary.

Transfer to a warmed serving dish.

130 BUTTER BEANS IN SESAME

Preparation time:
20 minutes

Cooking time:
25-30 minutes

Serves 4

Calories:
560 per portion

YOU WILL NEED:
120 ml/4 fl oz oil
1 teaspoon cumin seeds
1 large onion, chopped
100 g/4 oz sesame seeds, finely ground
1 tablespoon ground coriander
1 x 400 g/14 oz can tomatoes, chopped
   with the juice
2 teaspoons salt
2 teaspoons sugar
1 teaspoon chilli powder
1 teaspoon turmeric
2 x 425 g/15 oz cans butter beans,
   drained
2 sprigs fresh coriander leaves, chopped,
   to garnish

Heat the oil in a pan, add the cumin seeds and fry until they begin to crackle. Add the onion and fry until soft. Add the ground sesame seeds and fry for 3-5 minutes, then add the ground coriander and fry for a further minute. Stir in the tomatoes, salt, sugar, chilli powder and turmeric. Mix well and cook the sauce for 3-5 minutes. Add the drained beans and stir carefully until well coated with the sauce. Simmer until the beans are thoroughly hot. Sprinkle with chopped coriander and serve.

◼ COOK'S TIP

Dhal Sag, from northern India, is usually served with Chapatis (recipe 186). For an even more filling dish add 225 g/8 oz cubed potatoes before the spinach.

◼ COOK'S TIP

These beans are known as lima beans when they are fresh, and as butter beans when dried. Their slightly dry texture absorbs other flavours well, which makes
them particularly well suited for use in curries and other highly spiced dishes.

131 SPICY TURNIPS

Preparation time:
20 minutes

Cooking time:
about 20 minutes

Serves 4-6

Calories:
260-180 per portion

YOU WILL NEED:
about 3 tablespoons ghee or
concentrated butter
1 kg/2 lb turnips, peeled and quartered
2 garlic cloves, peeled
2 green chillies
1 x 2.5 cm/1 inch piece root ginger,
peeled
1 teaspoon cumin seeds
2 teaspoons coriander seeds
2 tablespoons natural yogurt
1 teaspoon salt
150 ml/¼ pint water
1 teaspoon sugar
1 teaspoon garam masala

Heat the ghee in a pan, add the turnips and fry lightly then set aside.

Put the garlic, chillies, ginger, cumin, coriander and yogurt into a liquidizer or food processor and work to a paste. Add to the pan and fry for 2 minutes.

Return the turnips to the pan, add the salt and stir well. Add the water and simmer, covered, for about 10 minutes, until almost tender. Uncover the pan, add the sugar and garam masala and cook briskly, stirring until most of the liquid has evaporated.

132 DAM ALOO

Preparation time:
20 minutes

Cooking time:
about 30 minutes

Serves 4-6

Calories:
250-170 per portion

YOU WILL NEED:
450 g/1 lb small potatoes, preferably
new
1 medium onion
4 tablespoons oil
about 1 teaspoon chilli powder
½ teaspoon turmeric
25 g/1 oz root ginger, peeled and ground
to a paste, or 1 teaspoon ground
ginger
½ teaspoon sugar
salt
150 ml/¼ pint water
1½ teaspoons garam masala
chopped coriander leaves, to garnish

Scrub or peel the potatoes and cut them into even-sized pieces. Boil them until just tender.

Grind the onion to a fine paste. Heat the oil in a pan, add the onion paste and fry until lightly browned. Stir in the chilli powder, turmeric, ginger, sugar and salt. Fry for 1-2 minutes without letting the mixture burn, then add the water. When the water begins to simmer, stir in the potatoes, cover and cook until the sauce has thickened. Sprinkle with the garam masala and remove from the heat. Garnish with coriander leaves and serve.

■ COOK'S TIP

Root vegetables such as turnips, swede, carrots and parsnips and tubers such as potatoes are excellent in spiced dishes because they absorb other flavours well.

■ COOK'S TIP

If necessary to prevent this burning and sticking to the pan during cooking, add a little extra water, and keep the heat low, too. Remember that it is a dry curry.

133 STUFFED BHINDI

Preparation time:
30 minutes, plus 12
hours marinating
time

Serves 4

Calories:
40 per portion

YOU WILL NEED:
450 g/1 lb tender okra
10 garlic cloves, finely chopped
6 green chillies, finely chopped
1 x 7.5 cm/3 inch piece root ginger,
  peeled and finely chopped
4 tablespoons finely chopped fresh mint
1 teaspoon salt
600 ml/1 pint red wine vinegar
sugar
mint leaves, to garnish

Top and tail the okra and slit them down one side.

Mix the garlic, chillies, ginger, mint and salt together thoroughly. Stuff the okra with this mixture and arrange in layers in a dish. Sweeten the vinegar to taste with sugar and pour over the okra to cover.

Cover and leave in a cool place for 12-24 hours for the flavours to mingle. Serve chilled with mint leaves.

134 THREE BEAN CURRY

Preparation time:
25 minutes

Cooking time:
30-35 minutes

Serves 4

Calories:
400 per portion

YOU WILL NEED:
100 g/4 oz butter
2 medium onions, finely chopped
3 garlic cloves, crushed
1 tablespoon ground coriander
1 teaspoon garam masala
1 teaspoon chilli powder
1 x 400 g/14 oz can tomatoes, chopped
  with the juice
salt
1 teaspoon sugar
1 x 425 g/15 oz can butter beans,
  drained
1 x 425 g/15 oz can kidney beans,
  drained
1 x 425 g/15 oz can haricot beans or
  cannellini beans, drained
5-6 sprigs fresh coriander leaves,
  chopped, to garnish

Heat the butter in a pan, add the onions and fry until lightly browned. Add the garlic and fry for a few seconds only, then add the ground coriander, garam masala and chilli powder and stir-fry for a few seconds. Stir in the tomatoes, salt to taste and sugar. Reduce the heat and simmer for 10 minutes.

Carefully add the drained beans, stir thoroughly then cover and heat gently. Garnish with the chopped coriander and serve at once.

■ COOK'S TIP

Serve this Bombay-style with plain fried chicken or fish and a dry curry, such as Dry Spiced Sweetcorn (recipe 143), Dam Aloo (recipe 132) or Aloo Gajjar (recipe 166).

■ COOK'S TIP

Red kidney beans must be heated thoroughly for at least 15 minutes. If using dried kidney beans, always boil them fast for the first 10-15 minutes of their long cooking time.

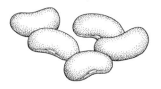

135 TAMATAR ALOO

Preparation time:
20 minutes

Cooking time:
15-20 minutes

Serves 4

Calories:
130 per portion

YOU WILL NEED:
2 tablespoons oil
½ teaspoon mustard seeds
225 g/8 oz potatoes, peeled and cut into small cubes
1 teaspoon turmeric
1 teaspoon chilli powder
2 teaspoons paprika
juice of 1 lemon
1 teaspoon sugar
salt
225 g/8 oz tomatoes, quartered
2 tablespoons finely chopped fresh coriander leaves

Heat the oil in a pan, add the mustard seeds and fry until they pop – just a few seconds. Add the potatoes and fry for about 5 minutes. Add the spices, lemon juice, sugar and salt to taste, stir well and cook for 5 minutes.

Add the tomatoes, stir well, then simmer for 5-10 minutes until the potatoes are tender. Sprinkle with chopped coriander leaves to serve.

136 GHASSEY

Preparation time:
10 minutes

Cooking time:
12-15 minutes

Serves 4-6

Calories:
240-160 per portion

YOU WILL NEED:
450 g/1 lb potatoes, preferably new, scrubbed but not peeled
40 g/1 ½ oz ghee or 4 tablespoons oil
4-5 garlic cloves, lightly crushed
2 teaspoons urhad dal
5-6 curry leaves
3 red or green chillies
salt

Cut the potatoes into very thin 2.5 cm/1 inch long chips. Wash thoroughly and drain well.

Heat the ghee or oil in a pan, add the garlic and fry gently until lightly browned. Add the urhad dal and curry leaves and fry gently for 30 seconds. Add the whole red or green chillies and fry for about 15 seconds. Add the chipped potatoes and salt and mix well. Cover and fry gently for 10-12 minutes until the chips are tender, turning them occasionally. If necessary a little water may be added during cooking. If preferred remove the garlic before serving.

COOK'S TIP

Many spices are dry-roasted in a pan or flash-fried for a few seconds to release their full flavour. Take care when flash-frying as mustard seeds will jump when heated.

COOK'S TIP

These dry chipped potatoes use urhad dal or black gram in their preparation. The pulses are available in Indian supermarkets and specialist shops.

137 COURGETTE CURRY

Preparation time:
15 minutes

Cooking time:
about 15 minutes

Serves 4

Calories:
600 per portion

YOU WILL NEED:
juice of 1 lemon
675 g/1 ½ lb courgettes, sliced
100 g/4 oz desiccated coconut
150 ml/¼ pint boiling water
175 g/6 oz ghee
1 large onion, sliced
2 garlic cloves, sliced
1 teaspoon mustard seeds
1 teaspoon onion seeds
1-2 teaspoons chilli powder
1 teaspoon freshly ground black pepper
1 teaspoon turmeric
100 g/4 oz canned tomatoes
1 ½ teaspoons salt
2 teaspoons garam masala

Pour the lemon juice over the courgettes and set aside. Immerse the coconut in the boiling water and leave for 5 minutes.

Heat the ghee in a pan, add the onion and garlic and fry gently until golden. Mix in the mustard and onion seeds and fry for 1 minute. Add the chilli powder to taste, pepper and turmeric and stir for 30 seconds. Add the courgettes and lemon juice, stir well, then add the tomatoes and salt. Bring to the boil, reduce the heat and simmer for 5 minutes, then add the garam masala. Cook for a few minutes until the courgettes are tender, then serve.

138 GOBI DHAL CURRY

Preparation time:
10 minutes

Cooking time:
about 1 hour

Serves 4

Calories:
290 per portion

YOU WILL NEED:
100 g/4 oz lentils
1 tablespoon oil
2 onions, chopped
2 tablespoons curry powder
1 tablespoon plain flour
600 ml/1 pint chicken stock
50 g/2 oz salted peanuts
25 g/1 oz desiccated coconut
2 tablespoons mango chutney
1 medium cauliflower, broken into florets
juice of ½ lemon
salt and pepper

Place the lentils in a pan and pour over cold water to cover. Bring to the boil and simmer for 5 minutes, then drain.

Heat the oil in a pan, add the onions and fry until softened. Stir in the curry powder and flour and cook gently for 2 minutes. Add the stock, peanuts, coconut, chutney and drained lentils. Bring to the boil, cover and simmer for 15 minutes.

Stir in the cauliflower, lemon juice and a little salt and pepper. Cover and simmer for 20-25 minutes. Serve hot.

■ COOK'S TIP

If you can obtain them, courgette flowers make a lovely – edible – garnish dipped in a light batter and deep-fried for a few moments.

■ COOK'S TIP

When boiling cauliflower on its own, you can help eliminate cooking odours by adding a little vinegar to the cooking water. Never overcook either cauliflower or cabbage – they should always retain some of their firmness.

139 CORIANDER TOMATOES

Preparation time:
10 minutes

Cooking time:
about 15 minutes

Serves 4

Calories:
160 per portion

YOU WILL NEED:
3 tablespoons oil
2 onions, finely chopped
1 teaspoon ground coriander seeds
1 teaspoon ground cumin seeds
½ teaspoon chilli powder
2 teaspoons finely chopped root ginger
1-2 garlic cloves, crushed
1 kg/2 lb tomatoes, sliced
2 green chillies, finely chopped
½-1 teaspoon salt
1-2 tablespoons chopped fresh coriander
    leaves
coriander leaves, to garnish

Heat the oil in a wok or large deep frying pan, add the onions and cook for 5 minutes until golden.

Lower the heat, stir in the spices and cook for 2 minutes, stirring. Add the ginger, garlic, tomatoes and chillies and stir well. Cook for 5-7 minutes until fairly thick. Season with salt to taste and cook for 1 minute.

Spoon into a warmed serving dish and sprinkle with the chopped coriander. Garnish with coriander leaves.

140 SPICED AUBERGINE

Preparation time:
10 minutes

Cooking time:
25-30 minutes

Serves 4-6

Calories:
140-90 per portion

YOU WILL NEED:
450 g/1 lb aubergines
40 g/1½ oz ghee or 3 tablespoons oil
1 large onion, finely chopped
25 g/1 oz root ginger, peeled and finely
    chopped
3-4 garlic cloves, chopped
about 1 teaspoon chilli powder
½ teaspoon turmeric
3-4 sprigs coriander leaves, chopped
1 green chilli, seeded and very finely
    chopped (optional)
salt
4-5 fresh tomatoes, skinned and
    chopped, or 1 x 225 g/8 oz can
    tomatoes

Prick the aubergines with a fork or skewer and cook them under a moderate grill for about 15 minutes, turning them frequently until the flesh feels soft. Allow to cool. Scrape off the burnt skin with a knife. Chop the flesh.

Heat the ghee or oil in a pan, add the onion and fry gently until just soft. Add the ginger and garlic and fry for 1-2 minutes. Add the aubergine flesh, and stir in the chilli powder, turmeric, coriander leaves, chilli, salt to taste and tomatoes. Fry for 10-15 minutes until dry. Serve at once.

■ COOK'S TIP

Coriander seeds are small round balls with a mild, slightly bitter taste. Cumin seeds are small half-crescent shaped seeds with a pungent taste. Both give a wonderful aromatic flavour to the tomatoes in the recipe above.

■ COOK'S TIP

Serve with Chapatis (recipe 186) and tomato butter, made by blending 100 g/4 oz butter with 2 teaspoons tomato purée and a pinch of caster sugar. Chill before use.

141 MASOOR DHAL

Preparation time:
15 minutes

Cooking time:
about 35 minutes

Serves 4

Calories:
350 per portion

YOU WILL NEED:
4 tablespoons oil
6 cloves
6 cardamoms
1 x 2.5 cm/1 inch piece cinnamon stick
1 onion, chopped
1 x 2.5 cm/1 inch piece ginger, chopped
1 green chilli, finely chopped
1 garlic clove, chopped
½ teaspoon garam masala
225 g/8 oz masoor dhal or orange lentils
salt
juice of 1 lemon

Heat the oil in a pan, add the cloves, cardamoms and cinnamon and fry until they start to swell. Add the onion and fry until softened. Add the ginger, chilli, garlic and garam masala and cook for about 5 minutes.

Add the lentils, stir thoroughly and fry for 1 minute. Add salt to taste and enough water to come about 3 cm/1¼ inches above the level of the lentils. Bring to the boil, cover and simmer for about 20 minutes, until really thick and tender.

Sprinkle with the lemon juice, stir and serve at once.

142 STUFFED CABBAGE LEAVES

Preparation time:
20 minutes

Cooking time:
35 minutes

Serves 4-6

Calories:
510-340 per portion

YOU WILL NEED:
1 cabbage
5 tablespoons oil
1 onion, chopped
1 x 1 cm/½ inch piece root ginger,
    peeled and chopped
1 teaspoon turmeric
450 g/1 lb lean minced lamb
75 g/3 oz long-grain rice
2 tomatoes, skinned and chopped
grated rind and juice of 2 lemons
2 teaspoons sugar
salt and pepper
150 ml/¼ pint water

Hollow out the stem end of the cabbage and discard. Place the cabbage in a large pan, cover with water and bring to the boil. Remove from the heat, cover and leave for 15 minutes; drain.

Fry the onion in 2 tablespoons of the oil until soft. Add the ginger and turmeric and fry for 1 minute. Add the lamb and fry briefly until brown. Cool slightly, then mix with the remaining ingredients, minus the water.

Carefully remove 12 inner leaves of the cabbage. Divide the meat mixture between these, gently squeezing out and reserving any liquid. Shape each leaf into a packet. Heat the remaining oil in a large frying pan, add the cabbage rolls in one layer and heat through. Pour over the reserved liquid and water. Cover and simmer for about 30 minutes, uncover, turn over and cook for a further 5 minutes. Serve hot.

COOK'S TIP

Serve this with lassi, a cool yogurt-based drink. To make 4 servings, beat together 300 ml/½ pint plain yogurt, 1.2 litres/2 pints water, 50 g/2 oz caster sugar and a pinch of salt. Serve the lassi with ice cubes and grated lime.

COOK'S TIP

Most of the liquid should have evaporated from the dish towards the end of cooking – if it hasn't then increase the heat and cook uncovered for a few minutes.

143 DRY SPICED SWEETCORN

Preparation time:
15 minutes

Cooking time:
20-30 minutes

Serves 4-6

Calories:
180-120 per portion

YOU WILL NEED:
40 g/1 ½ oz ghee or 3 tablespoons oil
1 small onion, chopped
1 medium potato, cubed
2 green chillies, seeded and halved
5-6 curry leaves
175 g/6 oz sweetcorn
about ½ teaspoon chilli powder
1 teaspoon ground coriander
½ teaspoon turmeric
salt
1 x 225 g/8 oz can tomatoes
2-3 sprigs coriander leaves, chopped
1 teaspoon garam masala
lemon juice

Heat the ghee or oil in a pan, add the onion and fry until soft.
Add the potato and continue frying for 4-5 minutes. Add the
chillies and curry leaves and fry for 1-2 minutes, then stir in
the sweetcorn, chilli powder, ground coriander and turmeric
and fry for 3-5 minutes until the mixture is dry. Add salt to
taste and the tomatoes, cover and cook for 5-8 minutes until
the potatoes are tender and the sauce has thickened. Stir in the
chopped coriander leaves, garam masala and lemon juice to
taste. Serve hot.

144 KAANDA MATAR

Preparation time:
25 minutes

Cooking time:
25-30 minutes

Serves 4

Calories:
170 per portion

YOU WILL NEED:
50 g/2 oz butter
1 tablespoon cumin seeds
1 large onion, chopped
2 garlic cloves, crushed
1 x 500 g/19 oz can marrowfat
    processed peas, drained
5-6 sprigs fresh coriander leaves,
    chopped

Heat the butter in a pan, add the cumin seeds and onion and
fry until the onion is soft. Add the garlic and fry for a few
seconds only. Carefully stir in the drained peas. Reduce the
heat, then cover and heat through, stirring occasionally to
prevent sticking. Add the chopped coriander, toss and serve
immediately.

COOK'S TIP

Serve this as a side dish with
a meat curry, or as a light
meal with Chapatis (recipe
186) and a rice dish. Add
sliced green pepper with the
sweetcorn if you like it.

COOK'S TIP

Most vegetable curries are
suitable for freezing, but not
those which contain potatoes.
This dish can be frozen, but
leave out the chopped
coriander leaves.

145 VEGETABLE CURRY

Preparation time:
15 minutes

Cooking time:
20-25 minutes

Serves 4

Calories:
100 per portion

YOU WILL NEED:
25-40 g/1-1½ oz ghee or 2-3 tablespoons oil
1 small onion, chopped
450 g/1 lb diced mixed vegetables (potatoes, carrots, swede, peas, beans or cauliflower, for example)
about 1 teaspoon chilli powder
2 teaspoons ground coriander
½ teaspoon turmeric
salt
2-3 tomatoes, skinned and chopped

Heat the ghee or oil in a pan and gently fry the onion until light brown. Add the diced vegetables and stir in the chilli powder, coriander, turmeric and salt to taste. Fry for 2-3 minutes.

Add the tomatoes, stir well and add 1-2 tablespoons water, then cover and cook gently for 10-12 minutes until the mixture is dry.

Serve as a side dish or as a main dish with rice or Naan bread (see recipe 192).

146 PHUL GOBI WITH PEPPERS

Preparation time:
10 minutes

Cooking time:
20 minutes

Serves 4

Calories:
140 per portion

YOU WILL NEED:
3 tablespoons oil
1 onion, sliced
½ teaspoon turmeric
1 cauliflower, broken into florets
salt
2 green chillies, seeded
1 green, 1 yellow and 1 red pepper, seeded and cut into strips

Heat the oil in a pan, add the onion and fry until soft. Add the turmeric and cook for 1 minute. Add the cauliflower and salt to taste, stir well, cover and cook gently for about 10 minutes until the cauliflower is almost cooked.

Add the chillies and peppers, stir and cook for a further 5 minutes until tender.

■ COOK'S TIP

This is the dry method for cooking a curried mixture – just a little water being added to prevent the vegetables from sticking to the pan. If a moister curry is preferred then 30 ml/½ pint water may be added with the tomatoes and simmered for 5-6 minutes until tender.

■ COOK'S TIP

Don't always use corn or sunflower oils, but try other varieties occasionally. Sesame oil has a lovely flavour and is traditionally Oriental, but it is comparatively expensive.

147 MATAR BATATA

Preparation time:
30 minutes

Cooking time:
25-30 minutes

Serves 4

Calories:
180 per portion

YOU WILL NEED:
50 g/2 oz butter
225 g/8 oz fresh or frozen peas
225 g/8 oz potatoes, diced
225 g/8 oz onions, diced
1 tablespoon garam masala
1 teaspoon turmeric
1 teaspoon chilli powder

Heat the butter in a pan, add all the ingredients and stir-fry for a few minutes to mix well. Cover and cook over a low heat for about 25-30 minutes or until the vegetables are tender. Stir occasionally during the cooking time to prevent sticking. Serve the dish hot.

148 KIDNEY BEAN CURRY

Preparation time:
15 minutes

Cooking time:
30-35 minutes

Serves 4

Calories:
350 per portion

YOU WILL NEED:
100 g/4 oz butter
2 teaspoons cumin seeds
1 large onion, chopped
1 x 400 g/14 oz can tomatoes, chopped
  with the juice
1 tablespoon ground coriander
1 teaspoon chilli powder
1 teaspoon salt
1 teaspoon sugar
2 x 425 g/15 oz cans kidney beans,
  drained

Heat the butter in a pan, add the cumin seeds and onion and fry until the onion is lightly browned. Stir in the tomatoes and fry for a few seconds, then add the coriander, chilli powder, salt and sugar and stir well. Reduce the heat and cook the sauce for about 5-7 minutes.

Add the drained beans, stir carefully but thoroughly and heat through for 10-15 minutes. Serve hot.

■ COOK'S TIP

Choose firm potatoes with an earthy smell, avoiding those with wrinkled skins. Pre-washed potatoes do not keep as well as unwashed ones. Store in a cool, dark place.

■ COOK'S TIP

Dried kidney beans can be used if you prefer. Soak overnight and then bring to the boil in fresh water. Boil briskly for 10-15 minutes before reducing the heat and *simmering as instructed on the packet until tender. Use the cooked beans as instructed in the recipe.*

149 INDIAN VEGETABLE MEDLEY

Preparation time:
15 minutes

Cooking time:
about 40 minutes

Serves 4-6

Calories:
200-130 per portion

YOU WILL NEED:
3 tablespoons oil
1 teaspoon fennel seeds
2 onions, sliced
1 teaspoon ground coriander
1 teaspoon cumin seeds
1 teaspoon chilli powder
2 teaspoons chopped root ginger
2 garlic cloves, crushed
1 small aubergine, thinly sliced
1 potato, peeled and cubed
1 green pepper, cored, seeded and sliced
2 courgettes, sliced
1 x 400 g/14 oz can tomatoes
2 green chillies, chopped
salt
50 g/2 oz frozen peas

Heat the oil, stir in the fennel seeds and cook for 1 minute, stirring constantly. Add the onions and cook for 5 minutes until pale brown. Lower the heat, add all the spices and cook, stirring, for 1 minute. Add the ginger, garlic, aubergine and potato, mix well and cook for 15 minutes.

Add the green pepper, courgettes, tomatoes with their juice, chillies and salt to taste. Bring slowly to the boil, then simmer, stirring occasionally for 10 minutes.

Stir in the peas and cook for 3 minutes. Transfer to a warmed serving dish and serve at once.

150 BRAISED OKRA WITH CHILLIES

Preparation time:
15 minutes

Cooking time:
15-20 minutes

Serves 4

Calories:
150 per portion

YOU WILL NEED:
50 g/2 oz ghee
1 large onion, sliced
3 garlic cloves, sliced
1 x 5 cm/2 inch piece root ginger, peeled and finely chopped
2 green chillies, seeded and finely chopped or minced
½ teaspoon chilli powder
450 g/1 lb okra, topped and tailed
200 ml/⅓ pint water
salt
2 teaspoons desiccated coconut

Melt the ghee in a large saucepan, add the onion, garlic, ginger, chillies and chilli powder and fry gently for 4-5 minutes until soft, stirring occasionally.

Add the okra, water and salt to taste. Bring to the boil, then lower the heat, cover and simmer for 5-10 minutes until the okra are just tender, but still firm to the bite. Stir in the coconut and serve hot.

■ COOK'S TIP

Indian spices impart a marvellous flavour to meats, fish and vegetables. Buy spices whole and grind them yourself as required, to ensure optimum flavour.

■ COOK'S TIP

This recipe is known as Bhindi Foogath in India, a foogath *being a savoury vegetable dish, in which the use of ginger is an important factor.*

151 CELERY SAMBAR

Preparation time:
10 minutes

Cooking time:
1¼ hours

Serves 4

Calories:
280 per portion

YOU WILL NEED:

225 g/8 oz tur dhal (yellow pigeon peas), washed and drained

1 teaspoon salt

1 teaspoon turmeric

1.2 litres/2 pints water

½ head celery, cut into 5 cm/2 inch lengths

2 tablespoons desiccated coconut

3 tablespoons boiling water

½-1 teaspoon small dried red chillies

1 teaspoon ground cumin

2 teaspoons ground coriander

50 g/2 oz tamarind, soaked in 150 ml/ ¼ pint water

25 g/1 oz butter

pinch of asafoetida (heeng) (optional)

1 teaspoon mustard seeds

Put the dhal, salt, turmeric, water and celery in a pan and bring to the boil, then partially cover the pan and simmer for 1 hour.

Put the coconut and boiling water in a food processor or liquidizer and work for 20 seconds. Add the chillies, cumin and coriander and work until smooth. Stir into the dhal with the strained tamarind water and simmer for 15 minutes.

Heat the butter in a small frying pan, add the asafoetida, if using, and the mustard seeds. When the seeds begin to pop, tip the contents of the pan into the dhal mixture. Serve hot.

152 POTATO, PEPPER AND PEA CURRY

Preparation time:
10 minutes

Cooking time:
15-20 minutes

Serves 4-6

Calories:
230-150 per portion

YOU WILL NEED:

40 g/1½ oz ghee or 3 tablespoons oil

1 small onion, chopped, or 1½ teaspoons cumin seeds

450 g/1 lb potatoes, peeled and diced

about 1 teaspoon chilli powder

½ teaspoon turmeric

1½ teaspoons ground coriander

1 x 225 g/8 oz can tomatoes

salt

100 g/4 oz green peas

1 green pepper, seeded and sliced

200 ml/⅓ pint water

chopped coriander leaves, to garnish

Heat the ghee or oil in a large pan, add the onion and fry gently until lightly browned. Alternatively, fry the cumin seeds until they crackle. Add the potatoes and fry for 3-4 minutes. Stir in the chilli powder, turmeric and coriander, and continue frying for 1-2 minutes.

Add the tomatoes, salt, peas and pepper and stir well. Cover and cook gently for 1 minute, then stir in the water. Cook until the potatoes are tender. Garnish with chopped coriander leaves and serve.

■ COOK'S TIP

To keep celery crisp, prepare it as soon as possible after purchase. Trim and wash the sticks, then store in the refrigerator in a jug of iced water.

■ COOK'S TIP

If you want to remove the green pepper's skin, place it under a hot grill, turning occasionally, until the skin chars and rubs off easily. Rinse away the skin and seeds under cold running water.

153 SPINACH WITH TOMATOES

Preparation time:
15 minutes

Cooking time:
20-30 minutes

Serves 4-6

Calories:
530-350 per portion

YOU WILL NEED:
1 kg/2-2¼ lb fresh spinach
175 g/6 oz ghee
2 large onions, thinly sliced
2 garlic cloves, thinly sliced
150 g/5 oz root ginger, peeled
2 teaspoons chilli powder
2 teaspoons turmeric
2 teaspoons garam masala
2 teaspoons coriander seeds
1 teaspoon ground coriander
1 teaspoon cumin seeds
1½ teaspoons salt
2 teaspoons freshly ground black pepper
1 x 400 g/14 oz can tomatoes

Wash the spinach and cut it into strips about 2.5 cm/1 inch wide, removing any of the thicker stalks. Melt the ghee in a large pan, add the onions and garlic and fry gently for 4-5 minutes until soft.

Meanwhile, cut the ginger into strips about 3 mm/⅛ inch thick, add to the pan and cook gently for a further 5-6 minutes. Add the chilli powder, turmeric, garam masala, coriander seeds, ground coriander, cumin, salt and pepper, stir well and cook for 1 minute. Add the spinach and toss to coat in the spice mixture. Add the tomatoes with their juice and bring to the boil, stirring. Add enough boiling water to prevent the spinach sticking to the pan. Stir well and simmer for 5-10 minutes, until both the spinach and tomatoes are cooked through. Serve hot.

◼ COOK'S TIP

Frozen spinach can be used if fresh is not available, in which case use only half the weight specified for fresh.

154 DRY TURNIP CURRY

Preparation time:
10 minutes

Cooking time:
about 20 minutes

Serves 4

Calories:
200 per portion

YOU WILL NEED:
450 g/1 lb turnips, peeled
50 g/2 oz ghee or 75 g/3 oz butter
1 onion, sliced
1 green chilli, seeded and finely chopped
1 teaspoon garam masala
salt
about ¼ teaspoon sugar (optional)
juice of 1 lemon

Slice the turnips into rounds and cook in 50 ml/2 fl oz boiling water until tender and dry.

Heat the ghee or butter in a pan and fry the onion until light brown. Add the chilli, turnips, garam masala and salt to taste. Taste and add the sugar, if it is being used. Cook for about 5 minutes.

Serve hot as a side dish, sprinkled with lemon juice.

◼ COOK'S TIP

This recipe can also be used to cook other root vegetables like swede and carrots.

155 BEAN KI TARKARI

Preparation time:
5 minutes

Cooking time:
20-30 minutes

Serves 4-6

Calories:
210-140 per portion

YOU WILL NEED:
50 g/2 oz ghee or 4 tablespoons oil
2 red or green chillies
2 teaspoons urhad dal, washed, soaked
  in cold water for 5 minutes and
  drained
6-7 curry leaves
175 g/6 oz potatoes, peeled and diced
350 g/12 oz sliced green beans
salt
1 tablespoon desiccated coconut

Heat the ghee or oil in a pan, add the chillies, urhad dal and curry leaves and fry for a few minutes. Add the potatoes and continue frying for 5-6 minutes. Add the green beans, salt to taste and coconut. Cover and cook for 3-4 minutes. Stir and cook for about 5 minutes until the potatoes are tender.

156 POTATO AND COURGETTE

Preparation time:
15 minutes

Cooking time:
25 minutes

Serves 4

Calories:
160 per portion

YOU WILL NEED:
3 tablespoons oil
1 large garlic clove, crushed
½ teaspoon chilli powder
2 teaspoons ground coriander
1 teaspoon ground cumin
1 teaspoon salt
2 tablespoons water
450 g/1 lb courgettes, sliced
225 g/8 oz new potatoes, halved
1 tablespoon finely sliced red pepper, to
  garnish

Heat the oil in a pan and fry the garlic for 30 seconds. Add the spices, salt and water, stir well and fry gently for 2 minutes. Add the vegetables, stir thoroughly, cover the pan and cook gently for 20 minutes or until the vegetables are cooked, stirring occasionally.

Garnish with the red pepper to serve.

■ COOK'S TIP

You can fry 3-4 crushed garlic cloves with the black gram (urhad dal) if you wish; or substitute ½ teaspoon each of chilli powder, ground coriander and ground turmeric for the whole chillies, urhad dal and curry leaves if you prefer.

■ COOK'S TIP

Courgettes are at their best when 10-15 cm/4-5 inches long. Trim them, then slice for this recipe, or serve whole, sliced in matchsticks, stuffed or grated.

157 PUMPKIN CURRY

Preparation time:
25 minutes

Cooking time:
about 30 minutes

Serves 4

Calories:
220 per portion

YOU WILL NEED:
450 g/1 lb pumpkin
20 g/³/₄ oz tamarind pods
40 g/1 ¹/₂ oz ghee or 3 tablespoons oil
¹/₄ teaspoon cumin seeds
¹/₄ teaspoon mustard seeds
¹/₄ teaspoon fenugreek seeds
¹/₄ teaspoon onion seeds
¹/₄ teaspoon aniseed
3 medium potatoes, peeled and cut into chunks
about 1 teaspoon chilli powder
¹/₂ teaspoon ground turmeric
1 teaspoon ground coriander
salt
1 teaspoon sugar

Peel the pumpkin in alternate strips so as to keep the flesh intact during cooking and cut into cubes. Wash and drain well.

Soak the tamarind pods in a cup of hot water for 10-15 minutes and extract the pulp. Repeat the process to extract any remaining pulp.

Heat the ghee or oil in a pan and fry the cumin, mustard seeds, fenugreek, onion seeds and aniseed for 30 seconds, then add the potatoes and fry for 2-3 minutes. Add the pumpkin cubes, stir well and fry for 4-5 minutes.

Stir in the chilli powder, turmeric, coriander, salt to taste and sugar, and continue frying for 5-6 minutes. Add the tamarind pulp, cover and cook until the potatoes are tender. Serve hot.

■ COOK'S TIP

Pumpkins and other squashes absorb other flavours well, particularly garlic and spices. Pumpkin is also nutritious, being high in vitamin A.

158 MATAR DAAL

Preparation time:
15 minutes, plus overnight soaking

Cooking time:
35-45 minutes

Serves 4

Calories:
310 per portion

YOU WILL NEED:
50 ml/2 fl oz oil
2 teaspoons black mustard seeds
a good pinch of asafoetida (optional)
225 g/8 oz split peas, soaked overnight and drained
1 medium onion, sliced
1 tablespoon ground coriander
2 teaspoons salt
300 ml/¹/₂ pint water
2 sprigs fresh coriander leaves, to garnish

Heat the oil in a pan, add the mustard seeds and fry until they begin to pop. Add the asafoetida, if using, and immediately stir in the peas. Add the onion, ground coriander, salt and water. Partially cover the pan and cook over a low heat for 35-45 minutes until the peas are tender but still remain whole. Stir occasionally to prevent sticking. Garnish with the sprigs of coriander and serve at once.

■ COOK'S TIP

Split peas are available in yellow and green varieties. They can be made into a purée for serving with other vegetables, or the two coloured varieties can be cooked until tender, mixed together with a vinaigrette dressing when cold and served with other salads.

159 AUBERGINE WITH TOMATOES

Preparation time:
15 minutes

Cooking time:
30-35 minutes

Serves 4-6

Calories:
480-320 per portion

YOU WILL NEED:
750 g/1½ lb aubergines, sliced
juice of 1 lemon
175 g/6 oz ghee
2 medium onions, thinly sliced
4 garlic cloves, thinly sliced
1 x 7.5 cm/3 inch piece root ginger,
    peeled and thinly sliced
2 teaspoons black onion seeds
1 x 7.5 cm/3 inch piece cinnamon stick
2 teaspoons coriander seeds
2 teaspoons cumin seeds
salt and pepper
2 teaspoons garam masala
1½ teaspoons turmeric
1 teaspoon chilli powder
1 x 400 g/14 oz can tomatoes
100 g/4 oz tomato purée
600 ml/1 pint boiling water

Prepare the aubergines (see recipe 164). Place in a bowl and mix with the lemon juice.

Melt the ghee in a large pan, add the onions, garlic and ginger and fry gently for 4-5 minutes until soft. Add the onion seeds, cinnamon, coriander and cumin and stir well. Fry for a further 2 minutes, then stir in the salt, pepper, garam masala, turmeric and chilli powder. Add the tomatoes with their juice and the tomato purée, stir well and bring to the boil. Add the boiling water, aubergines and lemon juice. Bring to the boil, then simmer gently for 15-20 minutes until soft.

COOK'S TIP

Black onion seeds (known in India as kalonji) are small, teardrop-shaped seeds used to add flavour to vegetable curries and Indian breads.

160 GOBHI MASALA

Preparation time:
20 minutes

Cooking time:
about 30 minutes

Serves 4

Calories:
220 per portion

YOU WILL NEED:
1 large cauliflower
1 bay leaf
4 cardamoms
1 clove
1 cinnamon stick
1 tablespoon mustard seeds
2 tablespoons poppy seeds
2 onions, chopped
50 g/2 oz root ginger, grated
2 garlic cloves, crushed
½ teaspoon turmeric
3 tablespoons tomato purée
50 g/2 oz butter
4 green chillies, chopped
450 g/1 lb tomatoes, quartered
300 ml/½ pint natural yogurt

Divide the cauliflower into florets and steam for 15 minutes.

Place the bay leaf, cardamoms, clove, cinnamon, mustard and poppy seeds in a small pan and roast over a low heat until they give off a strong aroma. Cool slightly, then grind to a powder. Add half the onion, ginger and garlic and work to a smooth paste. Mix in the turmeric.

Mix the tomato purée with 150 ml/¼ pint water. Melt the butter in a pan, add the remaining chopped onions and chillies and cook until soft. Stir in the paste and cook 5 minutes.

Add the tomatoes to the tomato liquid. Bring to the boil and simmer 5 minutes. Stir in the yogurt and cauliflower thoroughly. Cover and simmer gently for 15 minutes.

COOK'S TIP

Take care when roasting the spices in the frying pan that they do not overcook or they will taste very bitter when ground.

161 KAANDA BATATA

Preparation time:
25 minutes

Cooking time:
25-30 minutes

Serves 4

Calories:
290 per portion

YOU WILL NEED:
50 ml/ 2 fl oz oil
1 teaspoon black mustard seeds
750 g/1 ½ lb potatoes, cubed
1 large onion, sliced
1 teaspoon ground coriander
1 teaspoon chilli powder
1 teaspoon turmeric
salt
600 ml/1 pint water

Heat the oil in a pan, add the mustard seeds and fry until they pop. Reduce the heat and carefully add the remaining ingredients except the water and toss to mix well. Add the water gradually, stirring carefully, increase the heat slightly, then cover and cook until the potatoes are just tender.

Before serving lift out a few pieces of potato and mash them. Return the mashed potatoes to the pan and stir thoroughly to thicken the sauce. Serve hot.

162 MOONG GUJARATI

Preparation time:
10-15 minutes

Cooking time:
1 ¼ hours

Serves 4

Calories:
260 per portion

YOU WILL NEED:
1.2 litres/2 pints water
225 g/8 oz mung beans
3 tablespoons oil
1 teaspoon black mustard seeds
2 teaspoons cumin seeds
a good pinch of asafoetida (optional)
1 x 400 g/14 oz can tomatoes, chopped
    with the juice
1 tablespoon ground coriander
1 green chilli, seeded and halved
2 teaspoons salt
2 ½ teaspoons sugar
5-6 sprigs fresh coriander leaves,
    chopped

Place the water and beans in a saucepan. Bring to the boil, then lower the heat. Cover and simmer for 45 minutes until the beans are tender and have split open.

In a separate pan heat the oil, add the mustard and cumin seeds and fry until they begin to crackle. Add the as foetida, if using, and immediately add the cooked beans and stir, being careful not to spatter the hot oil. Add the remaining ingredients and stir thoroughly. Cover and cook for 25-30 minutes over a low heat, stirring occasionally to prevent sticking. Serve the dish hot.

■ COOK'S TIP

Serve this mild curry with a dry meat curry such as Bholar Gosht (recipe 69), or with Stuffed Bhindi (recipe 133) or Vegetable Curry (recipe 145).

■ COOK'S TIP

This mild curry makes a good, nutritious vegetarian meal, served with natural yogurt mixed with finely chopped plum tomatoes or cucumber, and a rice dish.

163 LENTIL COCONUT CURRY

Preparation time:
20 minutes

Cooking time:
55 minutes

Serves 4

Calories:
410 per portion

YOU WILL NEED:
40 g/1½ oz butter
3 onions, finely chopped
2 garlic cloves, finely chopped
1 tablespoon grated root ginger
2-4 green chillies, finely chopped
1 teaspoon turmeric
225 g/8 oz moong dhal lentils, washed
    and drained
1.2 litres/2 pints water
salt
50 g/2 oz creamed coconut
juice of 1 lemon
finely sliced green chilli rings, to garnish

Melt the butter in a large pan, add the onions, garlic, ginger and chillies and fry gently, stirring until soft.

Stir in the turmeric and immediately add the dhal. Fry, stirring, for 1 minute. Pour in the water, add salt to taste and bring to the boil, then partially cover the pan and simmer gently for 40 minutes.

Add the coconut and stir until dissolved, then stir in the lemon juice. Taste and adjust the seasoning if necessary, cover the pan and simmer for 10 minutes.

Transfer to a warmed serving dish and garnish with the chilli rings.

164 BRINJAL AND POTATO CURRY

Preparation time:
25 minutes

Cooking time:
30 minutes

Serves 4

Calories:
180 per portion

YOU WILL NEED:
350 g/12 oz aubergine, cubed
2 teaspoons salt
3 tablespoons oil
1-2 teaspoons chilli powder
1 teaspoon turmeric
2 teaspoons ground cumin
2 teaspoons ground coriander
1 x 2.5 cm/1 inch piece root ginger,
    peeled and finely chopped
350 g/12 oz potatoes, peeled and cubed
1 x 227 g/8 oz can tomatoes, sieved
juice of 1 lemon
2 tablespoons chopped fresh coriander
    leaves
1 teaspoon garam masala
lime slices, to garnish

Sprinkle the aubergine with 1 teaspoon of the salt, place in a colander and set aside for 20 minutes.

Heat the oil in a pan, add the chilli powder, turmeric, cumin, ground coriander and ginger and fry for 2 minutes. Add the potatoes and drained aubergine and fry, stirring, for 2 minutes.

Add the tomatoes, lemon juice, chopped coriander and remaining salt. Cover and simmer for 25 minutes or until the vegetables are tender. Just before serving stir in the garam masala. Garnish with lime slices to serve.

▮ COOK'S TIP

This dish is suitable for freezing. Remember that spices develop their flavours during freezing, so frozen curries are best eaten within a month.

▮ COOK'S TIP

Brinjal and Potato Curry is an example of a curry made with a combination of vegetables. If the sauce starts to dry out too much during the latter stage of cooking,
add a little water to prevent burning. It is delicious with Puri (see recipe 191).

165 SPICY FRIED OKRA

Preparation time:
15 minutes

Cooking time:
about 15 minutes

Serves 4

Calories:
230 per portion

YOU WILL NEED:
3 tablespoons ghee
1 large onion, sliced
2 garlic cloves, sliced
1 tablespoon ground coriander
1 teaspoon turmeric
½ teaspoon salt
½ teaspoon freshly ground black pepper
*450 g/1 lb okra, trimmed and cut into
   1 cm/½ inch pieces*
150 ml/¼ pint water
½ teaspoon garam masala

Melt the ghee in a pan, add the onion and garlic and fry until soft. Add the spices and seasonings, except the garam masala and fry for a further 3 minutes, stirring constantly. Add the okra, then stir gently to coat with the spice mixture, taking care not to break them.

Stir in the water and bring to the boil. Lower the heat, cover and simmer for 5-10 minutes until the okra are just tender, but still firm to the bite. Stir in the garam masala and serve hot.

166 ALOO GAJJAR

Preparation time:
10 minutes

Cooking time:
15-20 minutes

Serves 4-6

Calories:
130-90 per portion

YOU WILL NEED:
*15-25 g/½-1 oz ghee or 1-2 tablespoons
   oil*
2 teaspoons cumin seeds
225 g/8 oz carrots, diced
225 g/8 oz potatoes, diced
about 1 teaspoon chilli powder
½ teaspoon turmeric
1 teaspoon ground coriander
salt
120 ml /4 fl oz water

Heat the ghee or oil in a pan, add the cumin seeds and fry until they crackle. Add the carrots and potatoes and continue frying for 5-6 minutes. Add the chilli powder, turmeric, coriander, salt and water. Cover and cook for about 5-7 minutes until the carrots and potatoes are tender and the mixture is dry.

▮ COOK'S TIP

Buy a head of garlic that feels heavy for its size. Choose firm bulbs with plump cloves – the closer the skin adheres to the bulb, the moister the cloves will be.

▮ COOK'S TIP

Salted butter used in cooking browns and burns faster than salt-free butter and tends to discolour food cooked in it. Ghee or unsalted butter are best to use when a good *colour and flavour are required.*

167 VEGETABLE BIRYANI

Preparation time:
35 minutes, including soaking time

Cooking time:
1 hour

Oven temperature:
180C, 350F, gas 4

Serves 4-6

Calories:
580-380 per portion

YOU WILL NEED:
450 g/1 lb Basmati rice, washed, soaked
    and drained
salt
3 tablespoons oil
1 x 5 cm/2 inch piece cinnamon stick
6 cardamoms
6 cloves
2 onions, sliced
2 garlic cloves, finely sliced
2 green chillies, finely sliced
1 tablespoon grated root ginger
1 kg/2 lb mixed vegetables, cut in pieces
1 x 400 g/14 oz can tomatoes

Par-boil the rice in plenty of boiling salted water for 3 minutes, then drain.

Heat the oil in a large pan and fry the cinnamon, cardamoms and cloves for a few seconds. Add the onions, garlic, chillies and ginger and fry until soft and golden. Add the vegetables and fry for 2-3 minutes. Add the tomatoes with their juice, and salt to taste. Cover and simmer for 20 minutes or until the vegetables are tender.

Layer the vegetables and rice in a casserole, starting and finishing with vegetables. Cover tightly and bake for 25-30 minutes until the rice is tender. Serve at once.

168 DRY CABBAGE CURRY

Preparation time:
10 minutes

Cooking time:
20-30 minutes

Serves 4-6

Calories:
160-110 per portion

YOU WILL NEED:
¼ teaspoon fenugreek seeds
1 teaspoon cumin seeds
½ teaspoon aniseed
½ teaspoon mustard seeds
½ teaspoon onion seeds
25-40 g/1-1½ oz ghee or 2-3 tablespoons
    oil
2 medium potatoes, cut into chunks
1 bay leaf
450 g/1 lb cabbage, chopped
about 1 teaspoon chilli powder
½ teaspoon turmeric
2 teaspoons ground coriander
1 teaspoon sugar
1 x 2.5 cm/1 inch piece cinnamon stick
3 small green cardamoms
3 cloves
salt

Mix together the fenugreek, cumin, aniseed, mustard and onion seeds. Heat the ghee or oil in a large pan and fry the potatoes for 4-5 minutes. Add the mixture of seeds and the bay leaf and fry for a few seconds. Stir in the cabbage, chilli powder, turmeric, coriander and sugar. Cover and cook gently.

Meanwhile, grind the cinnamon stick, if using, cardamoms and cloves to a powder. Alternatively, mix ground cinnamon into the powder. Sprinkle on to the cabbage, add salt to taste and mix well. Cover and cook for a further 8-10 minutes until the potatoes are tender.

■ COOK'S TIP

If you have a food processor then simply rough-chop all the vegetables using the knife attachment. Take care not to over-process the ingredients so that they become too fine.

■ COOK'S TIP

The mixture of seeds here is known as panch phoran. If you prefer, use 1 chopped onion or 2 teaspoons cumin seeds instead of the panch phoran mixture.

169 LENTIL CURRY

Preparation time:
10 minutes

Cooking time:
25-30 minutes

Serves 4

Calories:
420 per portion

YOU WILL NEED:
225 g/8 oz dried red lentils
450 ml/¾ pint water
100 g/4 oz butter
1 large onion, finely chopped
2 garlic cloves, crushed
1 x 50 g/2 oz piece root ginger, peeled
    and chopped
2 tablespoons ground coriander
1 teaspoon garam masala
1 teaspoon chilli powder
1 teaspoon ground cardamom
1 x 400 g/14 oz can tomatoes, chopped
    with the juice
1 x 75 g/3 oz can tomato purée
2 teaspoons sugar
15 ml/¼ pint water
sprigs fresh coriander leaves, to garnish

Place the lentils and water in a pan and cook, uncovered, over a gentle heat for about 20-25 minutes or until tender.

Heat the butter in a pan over a medium heat, add the onion and fry until golden. Add the garlic and ginger and fry for a few seconds. Add the spices and fry for 2 minutes, stirring continuously. Stir in the tomatoes and tomato purée and fry for a further 2 minutes. Add the sugar, water and salt to taste and stir well. Partly cover, and cook the sauce over a gentle heat for about 15 minutes, or until the sauce becomes thick and most of the liquid has evaporated. Stir the sauce into the lentils and cook for a further 5-10 minutes. Garnish with fresh coriander and serve.

■ COOK'S TIP

The sauce in which the lentils are cooked is a good basic sauce which you can use to make a number of fish, shellfish, meat, poultry and vegetable curries.

170 DHAI ALOO

Preparation time:
15 minutes

Cooking time:
about 25-30 minutes

Serves 4-6

Calories:
400-270 per portion

YOU WILL NEED:
4 tablespoons oil
1 onion, chopped
1 x 2.5 cm/1 inch piece root ginger,
    peeled and finely chopped
1 tablespoon ground coriander
2 green chillies, finely chopped
675 g/1 ½ lb small new potatoes
1 x 227 g/8 oz can tomatoes
100 g/4 oz raisins
salt
300 ml/½ pint natural yogurt
2 tablespoons chopped fresh coriander
    leaves, to garnish

Heat the oil in a large pan, add the onion and ginger and fry until soft. Stir in the ground coriander and chillies and fry for 2 minutes. Add the potatoes, stir well, cover and cook very gently for 5 minutes, stirring occasionally so they colour evenly.

Add the tomatoes with their juice, raisins and salt to taste and stir well. Increase the heat a little and cook, uncovered. As the liquid evaporates, add half the yogurt, a tablespoon at a time. When the potatoes have cooked for 20 minutes and are just about ready, add the remaining yogurt, a tablespoon at a time, lower the heat and cook for 2 minutes.

Sprinkle with the coriander leaves to serve.

■ COOK'S TIP

This makes a lovely light meal in its own right, served with a rice dish and bread, or with a fish or meat curry for a more substantial meal.

171 AVIYAL

Preparation time:
20 minutes

Cooking time:
about 20 minutes

Serves 4-6

Calories:
650-430 per portion

YOU WILL NEED:
flesh and liquid from 1 coconut
300 ml/½ pint boiling water
175 g/6 oz ghee
2 large onions, thinly sliced
6 garlic cloves, thinly sliced
100 g/4 oz root ginger, peeled and sliced
4 green chillies, seeded and chopped
1 teaspoon mustard seeds
1 teaspoon sesame seeds
2 teaspoons onion seeds
2 teaspoons turmeric
100 g/4 oz canned tomatoes
225 g/8 oz courgettes, sliced
100 g/4 oz French beans, trimmed
2 red peppers, seeded and sliced
100 g/4 oz carrots, cut into sticks
1 tablespoon garam masala

Slice half of the coconut flesh thinly and set aside. Grate the remainder into a liquidizer, add the coconut liquid and blend. Place in a bowl, pour over the boiling water.

Heat the ghee in a pan, fry the onions and garlic until softened. Add the ginger and chillies and cook for 1 minute. Stir in the mustard, sesame, onion seeds and turmeric and cook for 2 minutes. Strain in the coconut liquid, bring to the boil, add the canned tomatoes and vegetables. Return to the boil, cover and simmer for 5-10 minutes. Sprinkle in the garam masala and add the sliced coconut. Cook for 2 minutes then serve hot.

172 KIDNEY BEANS IN PEANUT SAUCE

Preparation time:
25-30 minutes

Cooking time:
25-30 minutes

Serves 4

Calories:
570 per portion

YOU WILL NEED:
120 ml/4 fl oz oil
2 teaspoons cumin seeds
100 g/4 oz fresh, unroasted peanuts, ground
1 large onion, chopped
1 x 400 g/14 oz can tomatoes, chopped with the juice
1 tablespoon ground coriander
1 teaspoon chilli powder
1 teaspoon salt
1 teaspoon sugar
2 x 425 g/15 oz cans kidney beans, drained, reserving the liquid from 1 can only
3-4 sprigs fresh coriander leaves, chopped, to garnish

Heat the oil in a frying pan, add the cumin seeds and fry until they begin to crackle. Add the ground peanuts and fry for a further 3-5 minutes. Then add the onion and fry for a further 2-3 minutes. Stir in the tomatoes and the remaining dry ingredients. Mix thoroughly, then reduce the heat and cook for 2-3 minutes. Add the kidney beans and blend in the reserved liquid. Stir, cover and heat through gently. Garnish with the chopped coriander and serve.

■ COOK'S TIP

Aviyal is one of the traditional dishes prepared for the feast of Onam which celebrates the rice harvest and return to earth of the mythical ruler Mahabali.

■ COOK'S TIP

If you prefer to use dried pulses rather than canned ones, it is worth cooking them in a pressure cooker to save time and fuel. By pressure cooking you can cut *the cooking time to about one-sixth of the conventional boiling time.*

RICES & BREADS

Rice tends to be eaten more in the southern part of India, and bread in the north. Eating the two foods together is somewhat frowned upon by Indians, but there is nothing to stop you doing so, if you wish. You may use Indian bread to scoop up food instead of using cutlery, if you prefer.

173 PLAIN FRIED RICE

Preparation time:
15 minutes

Cooking time:
30 minutes

Serves 4-6

Calories:
460-300 per portion

YOU WILL NEED:
75 g/3 oz ghee or butter
1 small onion, chopped
2 teacups long-grain American or
    Basmati rice, rinsed and drained
1 teaspoon salt
4 teacups water

Melt the ghee or butter in a large pan, add the onion and fry until golden. Add the rice and salt, and fry for about 1 minute. Add the water, cover and bring to the boil. Reduce the heat and gently stir the rice a few times. Cover and cook on a very gentle heat for 10-15 minutes until the water is fully absorbed and the rice is cooked. Do not stir during cooking. If the rice is not cooked by the time the water has been absorbed, add 1 tablespoon warm water and continue cooking, without stirring, until the rice is tender.

174 PRAWN AND SPINACH RICE

Preparation time:
35 minutes, including
soaking time

Cooking time:
50 minutes

Oven temperature:
180C, 350F, gas 4

Serves 4

Calories:
800 per portion

YOU WILL NEED:
450 g/1 lb Basmati rice
salt
½ teaspoon turmeric
50 g/2 oz butter
3 tablespoons oil
2 onions, sliced
3 garlic cloves, finely chopped
1 tablespoon grated ginger
1-2 teaspoons chilli powder
2 teaspoons ground coriander
1 kg/2 lb spinach, chopped
450 g/1 lb peeled prawns

Fill a large saucepan two-thirds full with water and bring to the boil. Add the rice, 1 teaspoon salt and the turmeric. Boil for 3 minutes, then drain. Stir in the butter.

Heat the oil in a pan, add the onions, garlic and ginger and fry until golden. Stir in the chilli powder, coriander and 1 teaspoon salt and fry for a few seconds. Add the spinach and cook, stirring, until soft. Stir in the prawns.

Layer the spinach and prawns with the buttered rice in an ovenproof casserole, beginning and ending with spinach. Cover tightly and bake for 30 minutes. Serve hot.

COOK'S TIP

To make egg fried rice, pour 2 beaten eggs over the rice when almost cooked. Do not stir until the rice is fully cooked and the water is absorbed.

COOK'S TIP

The only rice that must be washed before cooking is Basmati, which should be placed in a sieve and rinsed under cold running water until the water runs clear.

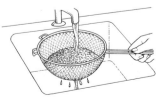

175 RICE WITH STOCK AND SPICES

Preparation time:
15 minutes, plus 30
minutes soaking time

Cooking time:
30-40 minutes

Serves 6-8

Calories:
650-490 per portion

YOU WILL NEED:
750 g/1 ½ lb Basmati or Patna rice
100 g/4 oz ghee
2 large onions, thinly sliced
4 garlic cloves, thinly sliced
2 x 7.5 cm/3 inch pieces root ginger,
   peeled
15 cloves
15 cardamoms
2 x 5 cm/2 inch pieces cinnamon stick
2 teaspoons turmeric
2 teaspoons black peppercorns
2 teaspoons garam masala
1 teaspoon salt
1.2 litres/2 pints hot chicken stock
100 g/4 oz sultanas
50 g/2 oz slivered blanched almonds

Wash the rice thoroughly, then soak 30 minutes; drain.

Melt the ghee in a large pan, add the onions and garlic and fry for 4-5 minutes until soft. Cut the ginger into strips about 5 mm/¼ inch x 5 cm/2 inches. Add to the pan and fry for 2 minutes. Add the cloves, cardamoms and cinnamon, stir well and fry for a further 1 minute. Add the remaining spices and salt and fry for a further 2 minutes, stirring.

Add the rice and stir well. Add the hot stock and bring to the boil. Boil gently, uncovered, until the rice is just hard in the centre, stirring occasionally; add a little more stock or water if necessary. Drain the rice. Transfer to a large platter and sprinkle with the sultanas and almonds. Serve at once.

176 SAFFRON RICE

Preparation time:
10 minutes, plus 30
minutes soaking time

Cooking time:
30-35 minutes

Serves 4

Calories:
720 per portion

YOU WILL NEED:
175 g/6 oz ghee
2 large onions, sliced
350 g/12 oz Basmati or Patna rice
1 teaspoon cloves
4 cardamoms
1 teaspoon salt
1 teaspoon freshly ground black pepper
½ teaspoon saffron threads, soaked in
   1 tablespoon boiling water for
   30 minutes
750 ml/1 ¼ pints boiling water
silver leaf (varak), to garnish (optional)

Melt the ghee in a large saucepan, add the onions and fry gently for 4-5 minutes until soft.

Wash the rice thoroughly, then drain. Add to the pan with the spices, salt and pepper, then fry for 3 minutes, stirring frequently. Add the saffron with its liquid and stir well to mix. Add the water, bring to the boil, lower the heat and simmer for 15-20 minutes until cooked. Drain. Transfer to a warmed serving dish and garnish with the silver leaf, if using. Serve hot.

■ COOK'S TIP

The addition of ghee helps prevent the rice grains sticking together. If you prefer, run a butter paper over the inside of the pan to prevent the rice sticking.

■ COOK'S TIP

Patna rice is grown in the Bengal and Bihar region of India, and is a good variety of long-grain rice to use if Basmati is not available.

177 COCONUT RICE

Preparation time:
35 minutes, including
soaking time

Cooking time:
20-25 minutes

Serves 4

Calories:
340 per portion

YOU WILL NEED:
350 g/12 oz Basmati rice
450 ml/¾ pint thin coconut milk
½ teaspoon turmeric
8 shallots, coarsely chopped
20 peppercorns
1 teaspoon salt

Wash the rice thoroughly under cold running water, then soak for 30 minutes; drain.

Put the coconut milk in a pan, stir in the turmeric, then add the rice. Bring to the boil, then cover and simmer gently for about 10 minutes. Add the shallots, peppercorns and salt and continue cooking gently for another 10 minutes or until the rice is tender. Be careful not to let the rice burn.

Transfer to a warmed serving dish and serve at once.

178 TOMATO RICE

Preparation time:
10 minutes, plus 30
minutes soaking time

Cooking time:
30-35 minutes

Serves 4

Calories:
330 per portion

YOU WILL NEED:
225 g/8 oz long-grain rice
3 tablespoons oil
1 onion, sliced
1 garlic clove, crushed
1 x 2.5 cm/1 inch piece root ginger,
    peeled and chopped
1 x 539 g/1 lb 3 oz can tomatoes
salt
2 tablespoons finely chopped coriander

Wash the rice under cold running water, then soak in fresh cold water for 30 minutes; drain thoroughly.

Heat the oil in a large pan, add the onion and fry until golden. Add the garlic and ginger and fry for 2 minutes. Add the rice, stir well and fry for 2 minutes. Break up the tomatoes in their juice and add to the rice with salt to taste. Bring to the boil, then cover and simmer for 15-20 minutes until tender. Transfer to a warmed serving dish and sprinkle with the coriander.

■ COOK'S TIP

*To peel shallots quickly, top
and tail them, and then cover
with boiling water for 5
minutes. Their skins should
then peel off easily.*

■ COOK'S TIP

*To crush garlic without a
crusher, place a peeled garlic
clove on a chopping board
and sprinkle with a little salt.
Crush with the flat, wide
blade of a knife.*

179 KITCHEREE

Preparation time:
15 minutes, plus 1
hour soaking time

Cooking time:
40-55 minutes

Serves 4

Calories:
580 per portion

YOU WILL NEED:
225 g/8 oz Basmati rice
225 g/8 oz yellow moong dhal lentils
1 garlic clove, sliced
5 cloves
5 cardamom seeds
1 x 5 cm/2 inch piece cinnamon stick
75 g/3 oz ghee
1 small onion, sliced
1 teaspoon turmeric
½ teaspoon salt
FOR THE GARNISH
fried onion rings
chopped fresh coriander leaves

Mix the rice and dhal together and wash thoroughly in cold water, then leave to soak in cold water for 1 hour.

Fry the garlic, cloves, cardamoms and cinnamon in the ghee in a large pan for 1 minute. Add the onion and fry for a further 1 minute. Drain the rice and lentils and add to the pan with the turmeric and salt. Toss gently over a low heat for 4-5 minutes.

Pour over enough boiling water to cover the rice plus 2.5 cm/1 inch, cover with a tight-fitting lid and simmer for 30-45 minutes until the rice is cooked and all the liquid has been absorbed.

Transfer to a warmed serving dish and garnish with fried onion rings and chopped coriander.

180 TAHIRI

Preparation time:
20 minutes

Cooking time:
30 minutes

Serves 4-6

Calories:
440-290 per portion

YOU WILL NEED:
50 g/2 oz ghee or butter
1 small onion, chopped
FOR THE GARAM MASALA
4-6 small green cardamoms
2-3 large cardamoms
6 cloves
1 bay leaf
1 x 1 cm/½ inch piece cinnamon stick
1 teaspoon black cumin seeds

50 g/2 oz peas
2 teacups Basmati rice, rinsed and drained
about 1½ teaspoons salt
4 teacups water

Melt the ghee or butter in a large pan, add the onion and fry until golden brown. Lower the heat and add the cardamoms, cloves, bay leaf, cinnamon and cumin seeds. Fry for 30 seconds and add the peas. Fry for 1 minute, then add the rice. Sprinkle with salt and stir gently a few times.

Add the water, bring to the boil and stir briefly. Cover and cook over a very low heat without stirring for 10-15 minutes until the water is fully absorbed. If the rice is not fully cooked by the time the water is absorbed, add about 1 tablespoon warm water and continue cooking. Transfer to a serving dish and lightly separate the grains of rice with a fork.

■ COOK'S TIP

Whole cloves give flavour and fragrance to apple pies, whole baked onions, soups, sauces, hot punches, curries and fruit compotes. A few go a long way.

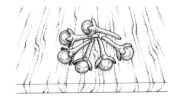

■ COOK'S TIP

If you like, use 50 g/2 oz mixed unsalted nuts and dried fruit instead of the peas in this recipe. Do not include cashews, almonds or pistachios if you vary the

recipe in this way as they contain strong, aromatic oils.

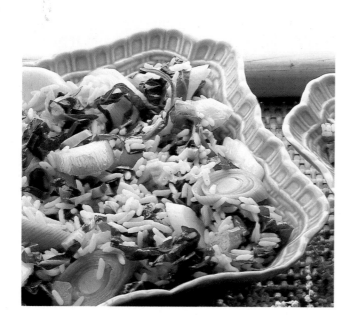

181 VEGETABLE RICE

Preparation time:
10 minutes

Cooking time:
15-20 minutes

Serves 4-6

Calories:
310-200 per portion

YOU WILL NEED:
2 tablespoons oil
2 leeks, washed and sliced
1 x 1 cm/½ inch slice root ginger, peeled
   and finely chopped
1 garlic clove, thinly sliced
225 g/8 oz long-grain rice
salt
225 g/8 oz spring greens, shredded

Heat the oil in a wok or deep frying pan, add the leeks, ginger and garlic and fry quickly for 30 seconds. Add the rice, stirring to coat each grain with the oil mixture. Add sufficient boiling water just to cover the rice. Season with salt to taste. Bring to the boil, cover and simmer for 5 minutes.

Add the spring greens, bring back to the boil and simmer for 7-9 minutes until the rice is tender. Drain and serve at once.

182 PLAIN BOILED RICE

Preparation time:
35 minutes, including soaking time

Cooking time:
20-25 minutes

Serves 4

Calories:
300 per portion

YOU WILL NEED:
350 g/12 oz long-grain rice
450 g/¾ pint water
salt

Wash the rice thoroughly under cold running water, then soak in cold water for 30 minutes; drain.

Place the rice in a pan with the water and salt to taste, bring to the boil, cover and simmer very gently for 20-25 minutes, until the rice is tender and the liquid absorbed. If cooking on an electric hob, the heat can be turned off once the rice has come to the boil.

Transfer the rice to a warmed serving dish. Serve as an accompaniment to curries and other spicy dishes.

■ COOK'S TIP

Substitute another green vegetable for the spring greens if they are not in season: perhaps add some pak-choi 4-5 minutes before the rice is tender.

■ COOK'S TIP

A quick and easy way to colour and flavour rice without using expensive saffron threads is to add ¼ teaspoon of turmeric for each ½ cup rice, adding it to *the water during the cooking time.*

183 PILAU RICE

Preparation time:
10 minutes, plus 30 minutes soaking time

Cooking time:
about 20 minutes

Serves 4

Calories:
310 per portion

YOU WILL NEED:
225 g/8 oz long-grain rice
3 tablespoons oil
1 x 5 cm/2 inch piece cinnamon stick
4 cardamom seeds
4 cloves
1 onion, sliced
600 ml/1 pint beef stock or water
salt
FOR THE GARNISH
lime or lemon slices
dill or fennel sprigs

Wash the rice thoroughly under cold running water, then soak in cold water for 30 minutes; drain.

Heat the oil in a pan, add the cinnamon, cardamoms and cloves and fry for a few seconds. Add the onion and fry until golden.

Add the rice and fry, stirring occasionally, for 5 minutes. Add the stock or water and salt to taste. Bring to the boil, then simmer, uncovered, for 10 minutes, until the rice is tender and the liquid absorbed.

Transfer to a warmed serving dish and garnish with lime or lemon slices and herb sprigs.

184 TURMERIC RICE

Preparation time:
20 minutes

Cooking time:
20-25 minutes

Serves 8

Calories:
370 per portion

YOU WILL NEED:
4 tablespoons oil
2 onions, thinly sliced
2 garlic cloves, crushed
450 g/1 lb long-grain rice
1 teaspoon turmeric
300 ml/½ pint coconut milk
1-2 stems lemon grass, bruised
salt
FOR THE GARNISH
1 chilli flower (see recipe 23)
1 plain omelette, made with 1 egg, cut into strips (see Cook's Tip)
cucumber chunks

Heat the oil in a large pan, add the onions and garlic and fry gently until soft. Stir in the rice and turmeric and stir well. Add the coconut milk and 900 ml/1½ pints cold water, then the lemon grass and salt to taste. Bring to the boil, cover and cook over a gentle heat for 15-20 minutes, until all the liquid has been absorbed. Remove from the heat and leave to stand for 15 minutes.

Mound on to a warmed serving plate, garnish with the chilli flower, omelette strips and cucumber chunks.

■ COOK'S TIP

Use this recipe to make vegetable pilau. Add 100 g/ 4 oz each shelled peas, sliced carrots and cauliflower florets after frying the onion. Fry 5 minutes, then add the rice.

■ COOK'S TIP

To make the omelette, crack the egg into a bowl, season with salt and pepper and beat lightly. Melt enough butter to cover the surface of a non-stick omelette pan and pour in the egg. When one side is set, fold the omelette over, remove from the pan and cut into strips.

185 CHICKEN AND CARROT RICE

Preparation time:
35 minutes

Cooking time:
35 minutes

Serves 4

Calories:
800 per portion

YOU WILL NEED:
1 teaspoon chilli powder
salt
3 chicken supremes, cut into strips
75 g/3 oz butter
2 garlic cloves, finely chopped
1 onion, sliced
50 g/2 oz split almonds
50 g/2 oz raisins
1 teaspoon turmeric
350 g/12 oz Basmati rice
450 g/1 lb carrots, grated
450 ml/³/₄ pint chicken stock

Mix the chilli powder and ¹/₂ teaspoon salt on a plate and lightly dip the chicken pieces in the mixture.

Heat 25 g/1 oz of the butter in a frying pan, add the chicken pieces and garlic and fry, turning them over constantly, for 2 minutes. Reduce the heat to low, cover and cook for 10 minutes until the chicken is tender.

Meanwhile, heat the remaining butter in a large saucepan, add the onion, almonds and raisins and fry until golden. Stir in the turmeric, then the rice and fry, stirring constantly, for 1-2 minutes. Add salt to taste, then stir in the carrots, chicken pieces and stock. Bring to the boil, cover tightly, reduce the heat to very low and simmer for 20 minutes until the rice is cooked and all the liquid absorbed. Transfer to a warmed serving dish and serve at once.

186 CHAPATI

Preparation time:
45 minutes, including
standing time

Cooking time:
12 minutes

Makes 12

Calories:
65 per chapati

YOU WILL NEED:
225 g/8 oz wholewheat flour
1 teaspoon salt
200 ml/¹/₃ pint water

Place the flour and salt in a bowl. Make a well in the centre and gradually stir in the water. Work to a soft, supple dough. Knead for 10 minutes, then cover and leave in a cool place for 30 minutes. Knead again very thoroughly, then divide into 12 pieces. Roll out each piece on a floured surface into a thin round pancake.

Lightly grease a griddle or heavy-based frying pan with a little ghee or oil and place over a moderate heat. Add a chapati and cook until blisters appear. Press down with a fish slice, then turn and cook the other side until lightly coloured. Remove from the pan and keep warm while cooking the rest.

Brush a little butter on one side, fold into quarters and serve warm.

◼ COOK'S TIP

Serve this with a meat curry such as Calcutta Beef Curry (recipe 54), or as a main dish on its own, accompanied by natural yogurt, relishes, and chutneys.

◼ COOK'S TIP

The Chapati is the daily bread of millions of Indians. It can be made from a mixture of white and wholewheat, or from barley, millet, maize or chick pea flour.

187 SAVOURY UNLEAVENED BREAD

Preparation time:
15-20 minutes, plus
20 minutes standing
time

Cooking time:
about 10-15 minutes

Makes about 12

Calories:
90 per portion

YOU WILL NEED:
50 g/2 oz ghee
100 g/4 oz strong plain flour
½ teaspoon salt
1 teaspoon lovage or caraway seeds
25 g/1 oz natural yogurt
2 tablespoons water
vegetable oil for shallow frying

Melt the ghee in a small saucepan until almost smoking. Sift the flour and salt into a bowl, then stir in the lovage or caraway seeds. Pour the hot ghee on to the flour mixture and mix well. Add the yogurt and cold water and mix to a moist dough.

Knead the dough in the bowl for 5-10 minutes, then set aside for 20 minutes or so. Turn the dough on to a work surface and roll out to a square about 2 cm/¾ inch thick. Cut into about 12 cubes.

Heat a little oil in a frying pan, add the cubes in batches and shallow fry for about 3 minutes until golden brown. Drain on absorbent kitchen paper and leave to cool before serving.

188 POPPADOMS

Preparation time:
about 30 minutes

Cooking time:
2-2½ hours drying
time then about
5 minutes

Oven temperature:
180C, 350F, gas 4

Makes about 20

Calories:
150 per poppadom

YOU WILL NEED:
450 g/1 lb urhad/lentil flour
4½ teaspoons salt
1 tablespoon baking powder
about 50 g/2 oz ghee
2 teaspoons black peppercorns
vegetable oil for frying

Sift the flour, salt and baking powder into a bowl and gradually add 250 ml/8 fl oz tepid water to form a very hard dough.

Melt the ghee, knead the dough for at least 20 minutes, sprinkling it with enough melted ghee to prevent it sticking. Crush the peppercorns and sprinkle over the dough, then knead until evenly distributed.

Break into about 20 pieces, roll out very thinly until 15 cm/6 inches in diameter. Stack on top of each other between sheets of greaseproof paper, then dry out in the oven for 2-2½ hours.

To cook, heat the oil in a deep frying pan until hot. Add the poppadoms, two at a time and fry for about 5-10 seconds, then turn them over and cook for a further 5-10 seconds (frying two together prevents them from curling up). Drain on absorbent kitchen paper.

■ COOK'S TIP

This can be stored in an airtight container for up to 1 week, and makes a tasty snack.

■ COOK'S TIP

The seeds of urhad dal are usually sold as lentils, and ground urhad dal is used to make this flour. It is sold in Indian supermarkets and specialist shops.

189 CHAPATI WITH ONION

Preparation time:
45 minutes, including standing time

Cooking time:
45 minutes

Makes 12

Calories:
100 per chapati

YOU WILL NEED:
225 g/8 oz wholewheat flour
1 teaspoon salt
about 200 ml/⅓ pint water
4 teaspoons ghee or unsalted butter, melted
2 onions
2 green chillies
½ teaspoon salt

Make the dough as for Chapati (see recipe 186), adding 2 teaspoons of the ghee or melted butter to the mixture.

Peel the onions, then chop the onions and chillies very finely. Stir in the salt. Place in a sieve and squeeze out any liquid.

Divide the dough into 12 pieces. Roll out each piece on a floured surface into a thin round. Put a little of the onion and chilli mixture in the centre, fold the dough over and form into a ball, then roll out carefully into a round.

Cook as for Chapati (see recipe 186), using the remaining ghee or butter to grease the pan.

190 PARATHA

Preparation time:
1 hour, including standing time

Cooking time:
15 minutes

Makes 6

Calories:
250 per paratha

YOU WILL NEED:
225 g/8 oz wholewheat flour
1 teaspoon salt
200 ml/⅓ pint water
50-75 g/2-3 oz ghee or butter, melted

Make the dough as for Chapati (see recipe 186) and divide into 6 pieces. Roll out each piece on a floured surface into a thin circle. Brush with melted butter or ghee and fold in half; brush again and fold in half again. Roll out again to a circle about 3 mm/⅛ inch thick.

Lightly grease a griddle or heavy-based frying pan with a little ghee or butter and place over a moderate heat. Add a paratha and cook for 1 minute. Lightly brush the top with a little melted butter or ghee and turn over. Brush all round the edge with melted butter or ghee and cook until golden. Remove from the pan and keep warm while cooking the rest. Serve warm.

◼ COOK'S TIP

You can flavour chapatis with any vegetable, providing you chop or mash it very finely and use only a little amount. Seeds, nuts and herbs are also good.

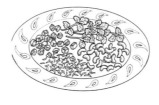

◼ COOK'S TIP

To make stuffed Parathas, roll one portion into a ball and made a depression in the middle. Press about 1 teaspoon dry vegetable curry into the depression and shape the dough into a ball enclosing the filling. Roll out into a circle and fry as above. Repeat until all the dough has been used.

191 PURI

Preparation time:
about 20 minutes,
plus 30 minutes
standing time

Cooking time:
about 5-10 minutes

Makes 16

Calories:
100 per puri

YOU WILL NEED:
225 g/8 oz wholemeal flour
¼ teaspoon salt
about 150 ml/¼ pint warm water
2 teaspoons melted ghee
oil for deep frying

Mix the flour with the salt in a bowl. Make a well in the centre, add the water gradually and work to a dough. Knead in the ghee, then knead for 10 minutes, until smooth and elastic. Cover and set aside for 30 minutes.

Divide the dough into 16 pieces. With lightly oiled hands, pat each piece into a ball. Lightly oil a pastry board and rolling pin and roll out each ball into a thin circular pancake.

Deep fry the puris very quickly, turning them over once, until deep golden in colour. Drain well and serve at once, hot.

192 NAAN

Preparation time:
2¼ hours, including
standing time

Cooking time:
10 minutes

Oven temperature:
240C, 475F, gas 9

Makes 6

Calories:
360 per naan

YOU WILL NEED:
15 g/½ oz fresh yeast
¼ teaspoon sugar
2 tablespoons warm water
450 g/1 lb self-raising flour
1 teaspoon salt
150 ml/¼ pint tepid milk
*150 ml/¼ pint natural yogurt (at room
 temperature)*
*2 tablespoons melted butter or cooking
 oil*
FOR THE GARNISH
2-3 tablespoons melted butter
1 tablespoon poppy or sesame seeds

Mix the yeast with the sugar and water and leave in a warm place for 15 minutes.

Sift the flour and salt into a bowl, make a well in the centre and pour in the yeast liquid, milk, yogurt and butter or oil. Mix to a smooth dough and knead for 10 minutes until smooth and elastic. Place in a bowl, cover and leave to rise in a warm place for 1-1½ hours.

Knead on a floured surface, then divide into 6 pieces. Pat or roll each piece into an oval. Place on warmed baking trays and bake for 10 minutes. Brush with the melted butter and sprinkle with the poppy or sesame seeds. Serve warm.

▣ COOK'S TIP

*These are delicious with
plenty of chutney or served
with vegetable curries. It is
essential – as with all Indian
breads – to serve them hot.*

▣ COOK'S TIP

*Naan – and Chapatis – freeze
successfully. Freeze the dough
or roll it out, interleave the
breads with cling film, seal
them in a bag and freeze.*

SALADS, PICKLES & EXTRAS

Offer a selection of accompaniments to complement the main dishes, with refreshing side salads for contrast and chutneys to enhance spicy dishes.

193 RAITA

Preparation time:
10 minutes, plus 30 minutes standing time

Serves 4

Calories:
40 per portion

YOU WILL NEED:
100 g/4 oz cucumber, thinly sliced
salt
300 g/10 oz natural yogurt
50 g/2 oz spring onions, thinly sliced
1 green chilli, seeded and finely chopped
fresh coriander or mint leaves, to garnish

Put the cucumber into a colander, sprinkle with salt and leave to drain for 30 minutes. Dry thoroughly.

Mix the yogurt with salt to taste and fold in the cucumber, spring onions and chilli. Arrange in a serving dish and chill until required.

Garnish with coriander or mint leaves to serve.

194 GUAVA AND YOGURT SIDE SALAD

Preparation time:
about 10-15 minutes, plus 1 hour chilling time

Cooking time:
about 2-3 minutes

Serves 6

Calories:
80 per portion

YOU WILL NEED:
300 g/10 oz natural yogurt
1 tablespoon lemon juice
3 canned whole guavas, drained, seeded and chopped
1 tablespoon ghee or clarified butter
1 teaspoon mustard seeds
1 green chilli, seeded and finely chopped
1 teaspoon chopped fresh coriander, to garnish

Beat the yogurt and lemon juice until smooth, then stir in the guavas.

Heat the ghee in a small frying pan, add the mustard seeds, cover and cook over a medium heat until the seeds begin to pop. Remove from the heat, add the chilli and then fry gently for 10 seconds, stirring constantly.

Stir the contents of the pan into the yogurt mixture. Cover and chill for at least 1 hour. Sprinkle the salad with the coriander before serving.

COOK'S TIP

Raita can be made with other vegetables and with fruit – bananas are particularly good. Other good garnishes include lemon balm, lovage, caraway seeds and pine nuts.

COOK'S TIP

Yogurt is much used in Indian cookery, particularly in savoury dishes. Try this recipe with fromage frais, live yogurt or thick Greek-style yogurt.

195 SPICY CHICKEN SALAD

Preparation time:
30 minutes

Serves 4-6

Calories:
110-70 per portion

YOU WILL NEED:
about 175 g/6 oz cooked chicken meat, shredded
1-2 tomatoes, peeled and chopped
freshly ground black pepper
1 green chilli, seeded and very finely chopped
½ cucumber, chopped
½ lettuce, coarsely shredded
1 small onion, finely sliced
1 green pepper, seeded and thinly sliced
1-2 sprigs coriander leaves, chopped
2 teaspoons cumin seeds
juice of 1 lemon
pinch of salt or black salt

Mix together the chicken and all the remaining ingredients in a large bowl or dish. If possible leave the mixture for 30 minutes before serving to allow the flavours to blend together.

196 MIXED VEGETABLE RAITA

Preparation time:
8-10 minutes

Serves 4-6

Calories:
100-70 per portion

YOU WILL NEED:
300 ml/½ pint natural yogurt
1-2 teaspoons freshly ground black pepper or chilli powder
salt
¼ cucumber, diced
1 small onion, diced
1-2 potatoes, boiled, peeled and cubed
2-3 tomatoes, chopped
100 g/4 oz radishes, sliced
1-2 sticks celery, diced
1 green chilli, seeded and very finely chopped (optional)
FOR THE GARNISH
1-2 sprigs coriander leaves, chopped
slice of radish

Beat the yogurt to a smooth consistency with the pepper or chilli powder and salt in a bowl. Add the vegetables and mix well. Sprinkle on the chilli, if using, and chill in the refrigerator. Garnish with coriander leaves and a slice of radish before serving.

■ COOK'S TIP

This makes a delicious light meal served on its own, in which case increase the quantities accordingly.

■ COOK'S TIP

You can also add a diced eating apple or other fruit to the Raita, or use soured cream, or French or Roquefort dressing instead of yogurt if you prefer.

197 ZALATA

Preparation time:
15 minutes, plus 30
minutes standing time

Serves 4

Calories:
10 per portion

YOU WILL NEED:
225 g/8 oz ridge cucumbers, peeled and
sliced
salt
1 green chilli, sliced
1 tablespoon finely chopped fresh
coriander leaves
2 tablespoons vinegar
½ teaspoon sugar

Put the cucumber into a colander, sprinkle with salt and leave to drain for 30 minutes. Dry thoroughly. Place in a serving dish and add the remaining ingredients and 1 teaspoon salt. Mix well and chill thoroughly before serving.

198 HOT RELISH

Preparation time:
10 minutes

Cooking time:
about 20-25 minutes

Serves 6-8

Calories:
130-100 per portion

YOU WILL NEED:
20 red chillies, seeded and chopped
10 shallots or 1 large onion, chopped
2 garlic cloves, chopped
5 macadamia nuts
1 teaspoon dried shrimp paste
2 tablespoons vegetable oil
1 teaspoon grated root ginger
1 teaspoon brown sugar
3 tablespoons tamarind water
salt
150 ml/¼ pint thick coconut milk or
cream (see Cook's Tip, recipe 2)

Put the chillies, shallots, garlic, macadamias and dried shrimp paste in a food processor or liquidizer and work to a very smooth paste.

Heat the oil in a pan, add the paste and fry for 2 minutes. Add the ginger, sugar, tamarind water and salt to taste. Stir well, then add the coconut milk or cream. Simmer for about 15 minutes until the sambal is thick and oily, stirring occasionally. Increase the heat and stir-fry for a further 2-3 minutes, then serve hot or cold.

■ COOK'S TIP

An alternative method to the one above is to put the drained cucumber into a liquidizer or food processor with the whole chilli, coriander leaves, sugar and

salt. Add 1 garlic clove and just 1 ½ teaspoons vinegar and work to a smooth paste. Chill thoroughly before serving.

■ COOK'S TIP

To chop onions or shallots, peel then cut them in half lengthways; place the flat side on a chopping board. Holding opposite sides, slice finely lengthways, then across.

199 PRAWN RELISH

Preparation time:
10 minutes

Cooking time:
about 15 minutes

Serves 4

Calories:
120 per portion

YOU WILL NEED:
2 tablespoons oil
1 onion, chopped
4 dried red chillies
2 green chillies, seeded and chopped
½ teaspoon cumin seeds
½ teaspoon turmeric
1 garlic clove, crushed
1 x 2.5 cm/1 inch piece root ginger,
    chopped
4 curry leaves, crumbled
150 g/5 oz prawns
1 tablespoon vinegar
salt

Heat the oil in a pan, add the onion and fry until golden. Crumble in the dried chillies. Add the fresh chillies, cumin, turmeric, garlic, ginger and curry leaves and fry for 2 minutes. Add the prawns and fry for 2 minutes. Add the vinegar and salt to taste and simmer, uncovered, for 3-4 minutes until most of the liquid has evaporated. Serve hot or cold.

200 COCONUT RELISH

Preparation time:
10 minutes

Serves 4-6

Calories:
110-75 per portion

YOU WILL NEED:
1 teaspoon dried shrimp paste, fried or
    roasted
2 garlic cloves, chopped
3-5 hot chillies, finely chopped
1 tablespoon gula jawa or palm sugar
    (see Cook's Tip)
1 tablespoon tamarind water
7 tablespoons freshly grated coconut
salt

Put the dried shrimp paste, garlic, chillies and palm sugar in a food processor or liquidizer and work to a very smooth paste.

Add the remaining ingredients, with salt to taste and mix well. Serve cold on the day of making.

■ COOK'S TIP

Ideally this should be made with freshly cooked prawns, but is still delicious made with pre-cooked prawns or even – if you're pushed for time – with frozen ones.

■ COOK'S TIP

Palm sugar, gula jawa, also known as gula malaka, is sold in thin blocks. Brown sugar may be used as a substitute.

201 CORIANDER CHUTNEY

Preparation time:
10 minutes, plus
1 hour marinating
time

Serves 4

Calories:
70 per portion

YOU WILL NEED:
25 g/1 oz desiccated coconut
150 ml/¼ pint natural yogurt
100 g/4 oz fresh coriander leaves and
some fine stalks
2 green chillies
juice of 1 lemon
1 teaspoon salt
1 teaspoon sugar

Mix the coconut with the yogurt and leave to stand for 1 hour to marinate.

Place in a food processor or liquidizer with the remaining ingredients and work until smooth. Chill the chutney before serving.

202 SAMBAL BAJAK

Preparation time:
10 minutes

Cooking time:
6 minutes

Serves 4

Calories:
90 per portion

YOU WILL NEED:
2 tablespoons oil
3 small onions, finely chopped
4 garlic cloves, finely chopped
1 teaspoon blachan or shrimp paste
100 g/4 oz red chillies, chopped
4 tablespoons tamarind water or lime
juice
1 teaspoon salt
1 teaspoon brown sugar

Heat the oil in a small frying pan, add the onions and garlic and fry until golden brown. Add the blachan or shrimp paste and fry, stirring and mashing, for 1 minute.

Stir in the remaining ingredients and fry, stirring, for 5 minutes or until the mixture is fairly dry.

Allow to cool, then spoon into a jar. Cover and keep refrigerated until required.

COOK'S TIP

Coriander chutney goes well with most curries and snacks and is excellent in chicken sandwiches. It is best eaten fresh, but will keep in the refrigerator for a day or two.

COOK'S TIP

Sambal Bajak comes from Indonesia, where the influence of Indian cooking has been considerable. It will keep for several weeks in a screw-top jar in the refrigerator. The

blachan or shrimp paste in the recipe is used throughout South-east Asia. Store in a tightly shut box. It must be fried or wrapped in foil and roasted before use.

203 TIL COPRA CHUTNEY

Preparation time:
10-15 minutes

Serves 4-6

Calories:
300-210 per portion

YOU WILL NEED:
100 g/4 oz tamarind pods
100 g/4 oz sesame seeds, dry roasted
100 g/4 oz fresh or desiccated coconut
1 green chilli, seeded and roughly
   chopped
3-4 sprigs coriander leaves, stalks
   discarded
1 teaspoon salt
1 medium onion, thinly sliced
a little water or lemon juice (optional)

Soak the tamarind pods in 4 teacups of hot water for 10-15 minutes and extract the pulp. Repeat this process to extract any remaining pulp.

   Grind the sesame seeds, coconut, chilli, coriander and tamarind pulp to a smooth paste. Add the salt and stir in the onion. If the chutney is too thick, add a little water or lemon juice or a mixture of both.

   Serve with a main dish, with savoury snacks or spread on slices of bread to make sandwiches.

204 APPLE CHUTNEY

Preparation time:
15 minutes

Cooking time:
about 20 minutes

Serves 4-6

Calories:
500-330 per portion

YOU WILL NEED:
1.25 kg/2 ½ lb cooking apples, peeled
1 tablespoon salt
500 ml/18 fl oz malt vinegar
275 g/10 oz soft brown sugar
100 g/4 oz raisins
100 g/4 oz sultanas
½ teaspoon mustard seeds
25 g/1 oz root ginger, peeled and sliced
1-2 garlic cloves, chopped
1 teaspoon chilli powder

Slice the apples, lay them in a dish and sprinkle with half the salt. Cover and set aside.

   Place half the vinegar in a pan, add the sugar and stir over a low heat until the sugar is dissolved. Bring to the boil until a thick syrup is made. Allow to cool. Place the remaining vinegar in a pan, add the apples and simmer for 3-4 minutes until tender. Allow to cool, then stir in the vinegar syrup, raisins, sultanas, mustard seeds, salt, chopped ginger, garlic and chilli powder. Bottle in airtight jars with vinegar-proof tops and allow the chutney to mature for 4-5 weeks before using.

■ COOK'S TIP

*If you wish, grind two garlic
cloves and add them with the
other ingredients.*

■ COOK'S TIP

*Try adding chopped mint
sprinkled over the top of the
chutney before serving for a
delicious accompaniment,
especially to pork dishes.*

205 BRINJAL PICKLE

Preparation time:
40 minutes, including
soaking time

Cooking time:
40 minutes

**Makes about 1.5 kg/
3 lb**

Total calories:
2400

YOU WILL NEED:

1 kg/2 lb aubergines, thinly sliced
1 tablespoon salt
300 ml/½ pint hot water
100 g/4 oz tamarind
50 g/2 oz cumin seeds
25 g/1 oz dried red chillies
50 g/2 oz root ginger, peeled and
  chopped
50 g/2 oz garlic, peeled
300 ml/½ pint vinegar
150 ml/¼ pint oil
2 teaspoons mustard seeds
225 g/8 oz sugar

Sprinkle the aubergines with the salt and leave in a colander for 30 minutes to drain.

Pour the hot water on to the tamarind and leave to soak for 20 minutes. Press through a fine sieve and set aside.

Put the cumin, chillies, ginger, garlic and 2 tablespoons of the vinegar in a food processor or liquidizer and work to a paste.

Heat the oil in a large saucepan and fry the mustard seeds until they begin to splutter. Quickly add the spice paste and fry, stirring, for 2 minutes. Add the aubergine, tamarind water, remaining vinegar and the sugar and stir well. Bring to the boil, then simmer for 30-35 minutes, until the mixture is thick and pulpy.

Leave until cold then pour into sterilized jars, cover securely with waxed discs and screw-top lids. Store in a cool place.

206 GREEN CHUTNEY

Preparation time:
30-50 minutes,
including soaking
time

Serves 4-6

Calories:
290-190 per portion

YOU WILL NEED:

50 g/2 oz tamarind pods, or 100 g/4 oz
  unripe mango flesh
175 g/6 oz fresh or desiccated coconut
4-6 large sprigs coriander leaves, stalks
  discarded
1-2 green chillies, seeded and roughly
  chopped
25 g/1 oz root ginger, peeled
1 teaspoon cumin seeds
½-1 teaspoon salt
1 small onion, finely chopped

Soak the tamarind pods in two teacups of hot water for 10-15 minutes and extract the pulp. Repeat the process to extract any remaining pulp.

Grind the coconut, coriander leaves, chilli, ginger, cumin seeds and tamarind pulp to a smooth paste. If using the mango, add a little water. Add salt and stir in the chopped onion. Serve with a main dish or with savoury snacks.

■ COOK'S TIP

This is a hot pickle that goes particularly well with chicken and beef dishes, such as Dry Chicken Curry (recipe 111), and Minced Beef on Skewers (recipe 58).

■ COOK'S TIP

Green chutney is popular in all parts of India. Apart from its use as an accompaniment, it can be spread on bread and used as a sandwich filling.

207 MANGO CHUTNEY

Preparation time:
10 minutes

Cooking time:
about 45 minutes

Makes about 1.25 kg/2½ lb

Total calories:
2,700

YOU WILL NEED:
1 kg/2 lb very firm mangoes
450 g/1 lb sugar
600 ml/1 pint vinegar
1 x 5 cm/2 inch piece root ginger, peeled
4 garlic cloves
½-1 tablespoon chilli powder
1 tablespoon mustard seeds
2 tablespoons salt
125 g/4 oz raisins or sultanas

Cut each mango in two lengthwise, slightly off-centre, so the knife just misses the stone. Repeat on the other side. Mark the mango flesh in a lattice without cutting through the peel. Cut the mango cubes from the peel (see Cook's Tip), and set aside.

Place the sugar and all but 1 tablespoon of the vinegar in a pan and simmer for 10 minutes. Place the ginger, garlic and remaining vinegar in a food processor or liquidizer and work to a paste. Add to the pan and cook for 10 minutes, stirring constantly.

Add the mangoes and remaining ingredients and cook, uncovered, for about 25 minutes, stirring as the chutney thickens. Pour into hot sterilized jars, cover with waxed discs, then seal and label. The chutney will keep for several months.

208 BANANA CHUTNEY

Preparation time:
30-50 minutes, including soaking time

Serves 4-6

Calories:
120-80 per portion

YOU WILL NEED:
50-75 g/2-3 oz tamarind pods
2 tablespoons sugar
50 g/2 oz raisins and sultanas
about 1 teaspoon chilli powder, dry roasted
15 g/½ oz root ginger, peeled and grated
pinch of salt
2-3 ripe bananas, sliced
1 teaspoon cumin seeds, dry roasted and ground
a little lemon juice or water (optional)

Soak the tamarind pods in two or three teacups of hot water for 10-15 minutes and extract the pulp. Repeat this process to extract any remaining pulp. Mix together the tamarind pulp, sugar, raisins, sultanas and chilli powder in a bowl, and stir until the sugar dissolves. Add the ginger, salt and banana. Sprinkle with the cumin powder. Add a little lemon juice or water to thin down the chutney if necessary.

■ COOK'S TIP

Holding the mango flesh upwards, carefully push the centre of the peel with your thumbs to turn it inside out.

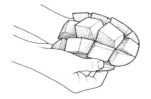

■ COOK'S TIP

You can add 225 g/8 oz dessert or dried dates to the chutney if liked. If using dried dates, soak them in warm water for 5-10 minutes. Remove the stones   *and slice the dates before adding to the mixture.*

209 BERTHA'S CHUTNEY

Preparation time:
5 minutes

Cooking time:
45 minutes

**Makes about 1.5 kg/
3 lb**

Total calories:
1700

YOU WILL NEED:
1 kg/2 lb tomatoes, quartered
100 ml/4 fl oz vinegar
225 g/8 oz sugar
100 g/4 oz raisins
100 g/4 oz sultanas
25 g/1 oz blanched almonds, sliced
4 garlic cloves, finely sliced
*25 g/1 oz root ginger, peeled and finely
    chopped*
1 tablespoon chilli powder
½ tablespoon salt

Place the tomatoes and vinegar in a large pan and heat gently until the juice starts to run. Add the sugar and bring slowly to the boil. Simmer for 5 minutes.

Add the remaining ingredients and simmer for 30 minutes until the mixture has thickened. Leave until cold, then pour into sterilized jars, cover securely with waxed discs and screw-top lids. Store in a cool place.

210 BRINJAL SAMBAL

Preparation time:
15 minutes

Cooking time:
30 minutes

Oven temperature:
180C, 350F, gas 4

Serves 4

Calories:
40 per portion

YOU WILL NEED:
1 large aubergine
1 small onion, finely chopped
3 green chillies, finely chopped
*1 x 1 cm/½ inch piece root ginger, cut
    into fine strips*
*2 tablespoons thick coconut milk or
    cream*
½ teaspoon salt
juice of 1 lemon

Place the aubergine on a baking tray and bake for 30 minutes or until soft. Leave to cool slightly, then slit it open and scoop out the flesh into a bowl.

Mash the aubergine with a fork and then mix in the remaining ingredients. Taste the sambal and adjust the seasoning. Serve chilled.

■ COOK'S TIP

*This chutney goes well with
curries and dhals, but is also
good with cold roast meats.
It will keep well if stored in a
cool, dry place.*

■ COOK'S TIP

*Brinjal Sambal is a typical
southern Indian relish. It is
quick and easy to make and,
for those who like the chilli-
hot taste, it makes an exciting
dip for raw vegetables.*

211 APRICOT CHUTNEY

Preparation time:
10 minutes, plus
overnight soaking
time

Cooking time:
about 55 minutes

Serves 4-6

Calories:
360-240 per portion

YOU WILL NEED:
*225 g/8 oz dried apricots, soaked
    overnight*
150 ml/¼ pint vinegar
250 g/9 oz sugar
*25 g/1 oz root ginger, peeled and
    crushed*
4 garlic cloves, crushed (optional)
about 1 teaspoon chilli powder
pinch of salt

Place the apricots and the soaking liquid with enough water to cover in a saucepan. Simmer until tender then beat or blend to a smooth consistency.

In a separate pan place the vinegar, sugar, ginger, garlic, chilli powder and salt. Heat gently, stirring, until the sugar has dissolved, then increase the heat until a syrup is formed.

Stir the apricots into the syrup and simmer gently for about 10 minutes to the desired thickness. Allow to cool and bottle in airtight jars with vinegar-proof tops.

212 YOGURT CURRY

Preparation time:
10 minutes

Cooking time:
25 minutes

Serves 4

Calories:
130 per portion

YOU WILL NEED:
450 g/1 lb natural yogurt
2 tablespoons gram flour
2 tablespoons oil
½ teaspoon ground cumin
½ teaspoon ground coriander
2 garlic cloves, crushed
3-4 green chillies, finely chopped
1 teaspoon turmeric
salt
*1 tablespoon chopped fresh coriander
    leaves*
6 curry leaves
fresh coriander leaves, to garnish

Mix the yogurt and the gram flour together.

Heat the oil in a pan, add the cumin, ground coriander, garlic and chillies and fry for 1 minute. Stir in the turmeric, then immediately pour in the yogurt mixture. Add salt to taste and simmer, uncovered, for 10 minutes, stirring occasionally.

Add the chopped coriander and the curry leaves and continue cooking for a further 10 minutes. Transfer to a warmed serving dish and garnish with coriander leaves to serve.

■ COOK'S TIP

You can use fresh apricots if the season allows to make this chutney, which is particularly delicious with lamb curries and chick pea dishes.

■ COOK'S TIP

This can be served as an accompaniment to a dry vegetable or poultry curry, such as Dry Okra Curry (recipe 128) or Dry Chicken Curry (recipe 111).

213 POACHED EGG CURRY

Preparation time:
10 minutes

Cooking time:
30 minutes

Serves 4

Calories:
230 per portion

YOU WILL NEED:
3 tablespoons oil
1 teaspoon mustard seeds
6 curry leaves
4 onions, finely chopped
2 garlic cloves, crushed
2-4 green chillies, finely chopped
1 x 3.5 cm/1½ inch piece root ginger,
    peeled and grated
1 teaspoon turmeric
1 tablespoon ground coriander
1 teaspoon chilli powder
salt
1 x 397 g/14 oz can tomatoes, sieved
4 eggs

Heat the oil in a large frying pan and add the mustard seeds and curry leaves. When the seeds begin to pop, add the onions, garlic, chillies and ginger. Fry, stirring constantly, until soft and golden. Add the turmeric, coriander, chilli powder and salt to taste and fry, stirring, for 2-3 minutes. Stir in the tomatoes and cook for 15-20 minutes; add a little water if the curry becomes too thick.

Adjust the quantity of salt if necessary. Break the eggs into the curry and cook gently until they are cooked to your liking. Serve immediately.

214 HOT SPICY EGGS

Preparation time:
15 minutes

Cooking time:
about 5 minutes

Serves 4

Calories:
450 per portion

YOU WILL NEED:
2.5 cm/1 inch cube dried shrimp paste
2 onions, coarsely chopped
2 garlic cloves, peeled
1 teaspoon laos powder
1-2 tablespoons sambal ulek (see Cook's
    Tip)
2-4 fresh chillies, seeded
4-6 tablespoons vegetable oil
3-4 tablespoons tomato purée
400 ml/14 fl oz stock or water
2 teaspoons tamarind, soaked in
    4 tablespoons warm water for
    10 minutes
2 teaspoons brown sugar
1-2 tablespoons coconut cream (see
    Cook's Tip, recipe 2)
salt
8 hard-boiled eggs, shelled
1-2 spring onion tops, shredded

Put the shrimp paste with the onions, garlic, laos powder, sambal ulek and chillies in a food processor or liquidizer and work to a smooth paste. Heat the oil and fry the paste, without browning, until it gives off a spicy aroma. Stir in the tomato purée and stock or water. Simmer, uncovered, a few minutes.

Just before serving, strain in the tamarind water, add the sugar, coconut cream and salt to taste. Leave the eggs whole or cut in half and add to the sauce. Heat through, then transfer to a serving dish and sprinkle with the spring onions. Serve hot.

■ COOK'S TIP

Deriving from an old Anglo-Indian recipe, this dish is good served with a variety of dressed salads such as cucumber and mint, or tomato and onion slices.

■ COOK'S TIP

Sambal ulek is a paste which can be purchased ready-made or prepared at home; 2 fresh chillies and ½ teaspoon salt pounded until smooth will make about 2 teaspoons.

Sambal Goreng sauce is also useful for other ingredients besides eggs. Try it with cooked green beans, cooked chicken livers or peeled prawns.

215 FRUIT SAVOURY

Preparation time:
15 minutes

Serves 4

Calories:
320 per portion

YOU WILL NEED:
2 eating apples, cored and sliced
2-3 bananas, peeled and sliced
1 pear, peeled and sliced
1 orange, peeled, pith removed, seeded,
   segmented and cut in half
1 x 425 g/15 oz can sliced peaches,
   drained
a few grapes
½ cucumber, chopped
1 x 425 g/15 oz can pineapple chunks,
   drained
1 x 425 g/15 oz can guavas, drained and
   lightly mashed
approx. ½ teaspoon chilli powder
salt and pepper
1 small ripe papaya (pawpaw), peeled,
   seeded and cubed
lemon juice, to taste

In a large bowl, mix together the apple, banana, pear, orange, peaches, grapes, cucumber, pineapple and guavas. Sprinkle with the chilli powder, salt and pepper. Add the cubed papaya and sprinkle with lemon juice. Toss all the fruits well together so that the seasonings are mixed through.

216 DRIED FRUIT CURRY

Preparation time:
10 minutes, plus
overnight soaking
time

Cooking time:
40 minutes

Serves 4

Calories:
220 per portion

YOU WILL NEED:
1 onion, peeled
1 garlic clove, peeled
1 x 2.5 cm/1 inch piece root ginger,
   peeled
2 teaspoons chilli powder
2 teaspoons ground coriander
1 teaspoon salt
2 tablespoons oil
225 g/8 oz mixed dried fruit, excluding
   prunes, soaked overnight
juice of 1-2 lemons

Place the onion, garlic, ginger, chilli powder, coriander and salt in a food processor or liquidizer and work to a smooth paste.

Heat the oil in a pan, add the paste and fry for 3 minutes.

Drain the fruit, reserving the liquid, and cut up the larger pieces. Add to the pan and fry for 2 minutes. Make up the reserved liquid to 300 ml/½ pint with water, add to the pan and simmer for 30 minutes.

Stir in the lemon juice to taste and serve at once.

■ COOK'S TIP

The combination of fruit and vegetables and contrasting flavours that are sweet and tart, spicy and refreshing, is typical of Indian cuisine. Serve this with any meat, *poultry or vegetable dish, or on its own with plain boiled rice.*

■ COOK'S TIP

Dried fruits, especially apricots, are very nutritious and good in curries. This is an excellent one to serve as an accompaniment to a lamb curry.

DESSERTS & SWEETS

Although desserts are normally served only at feasts and celebrations in India, and sweetmeats are eaten throughout the day as snacks, there is nothing to prevent you rounding off a meal, western-style, with an Indian pudding or sweet if you choose.

217 RICE PUDDING

Preparation time:
10 minutes

Cooking time:
1 hour

Serves 4-6

Calories:
520-350 per portion

YOU WILL NEED:
1 teaspoon ghee or butter
1 x 1 cm/½ inch piece cinnamon stick
100 g/4 oz coarse semolina or ground rice
1.2 litres/2 pints milk
175 g/6 oz sugar
25 g/1 oz sultanas
10-15 small green cardamoms, shelled and seeds ground
25 g/1 oz blanched almonds, sliced or chopped

Melt the ghee or butter in a heavy-based or non-stick pan. Add the cinnamon and fry for 30 seconds. Add the semolina or rice and half the milk and stir. Cover and cook for 15-20 minutes until soft.

Mash the mixture, then stir in the sugar and the remaining milk. Simmer gently for 20-25 minutes, stirring constantly to prevent the pudding sticking to the base of the pan. By this time it should be thick. Add the sultanas and check for sweetness. If the pudding is too thick, add a little extra milk or water and cook gently for 5-6 minutes.

Remove from the heat and pour into a serving dish. Stir in the ground cardamom and decorate with the nuts. This can be served hot or cold, and is especially good if chilled in the refrigerator before serving.

■ COOK'S TIP

This can be flavoured with saffron, vanilla or coconut milk, or sliced fruits such as bananas, oranges, dates, apples can be added w¹ the pudding has cooled

218 VERMICELLI PUDDING

Preparation time:
5 minutes

Cooking time:
20-25 minutes

Serves 6

Calories:
440 per portion

YOU WILL NEED:
100 g/4 oz ghee
100 g/4 oz vermicelli
750 ml/1 ¼ pints milk
15 cardamoms
225 g/8 oz clear honey
100g/4 oz sultanas

Heat the ghee in a heavy-based pan and add the vermicelli, breaking it into 4 cm/1½ inch pieces. Fry gently for 5-6 minutes, then pour on the milk and bring to the boil.

Remove the seeds from the cardamoms and crush in a pestle and mortar. Sprinkle into the pan and add the honey, spoon by spoon. Stir well until the honey has melted. Cook for a further 10-15 minutes, then stir in the sultanas. Serve hot or chilled.

■ COOK'S TIP

When Muslims visit each other on feast days, they are always asked to partake of some food. Invariably a large bowl of vermicelli pudding is offered to the visitors.

219 MIXED FRUIT SHERBERT

Preparation time:
15-20 minutes

Serves 8-10

Calories:
150-120 per portion

YOU WILL NEED:
about 100 g/4 oz caster sugar
300 ml/½ pint water
juice of 2 lemons
1.2 litres/2 pints lemonade
1 banana, sliced
1 orange, sliced and quartered
1 apple, quartered and thinly sliced
1 pear, quartered and thinly sliced
*2 rings fresh or canned pineapple, thinly
    sliced*
8-10 firm strawberries, hulled and sliced
few grapes, halved
*mint leaves, chopped or crushed by
    hand*
grated rind of 1 lemon
85 ml/3 fl oz gin or vodka (optional)

Dissolve the sugar in the water by stirring well. Add the lemon juice and lemonade. Add the fruit and stir gently. Add the mint, lemon rind and gin or vodka, if using. Mix well and serve chilled or with crushed ice.

220 FRIED BREAD IN SAFFRON AND PISTACHIO SAUCE

Preparation time:
15 minutes, plus
1 hour chilling time

Cooking time:
about 5 minutes

Serves 6

Calories:
630 per portion

YOU WILL NEED:
1 small loaf white bread, crusts removed
vegetable oil for deep frying
1 teaspoon saffron threads
600 ml/1 pint milk, warmed
225 g/8 oz clear honey
*50 g/2 oz shelled pistachios, coarsely
    chopped*
25 g/1 oz blanched almonds, chopped
300 ml/½ pint single cream
5-6 drops rose water

Cut the bread into 2.5 cm/1 inch thick slices, then cut each slice lengthways. Heat the oil in a deep fat frier and deep fry the bread until golden. Drain on absorbent kitchen paper and keep hot.

Put the saffron in a cup and cover with some of the milk. Add the honey to the remaining milk and heat until melted, then add the nuts. Strain in the saffron-coloured milk, stir and remove from the heat. Cool slightly.

Stir in the cream and rose water. Put the bread in the serving bowl, pour over the sauce and chill in the refrigerator for at least 1 hour before serving.

■ COOK'S TIP

A useful tool for removing grapeseeds is a clean hairgrip stuck by the pronged end in a cork. Use the rounded U-shaped end for hooking the seeds out of the grape flesh.

■ COOK'S TIP

Green pistachio nuts can be bought shelled or in their husks and can be used in a decorative way, as here, or served as a snack with pre-dinner drinks.

221 COCONUT PUDDING

Preparation time:
25 minutes, plus 15
minutes standing time

Cooking time:
about 40 minutes

Oven temperature:
180C, 350F, gas 4

Serves 4

Calories:
1,300 per portion

YOU WILL NEED:
2 fresh coconuts
450 ml/¾ pint boiling water
225 g/8 oz caster sugar
175 g/6 oz rice flour
2 eggs, beaten
50 g/2 oz slivered almonds

Prepare the coconuts (see recipe 121). Grate the coconut flesh
into a bowl, then pour on the boiling water. Allow to stand for
15 minutes, then strain the liquor through a sieve lined with a
double thickness of muslin held over a bowl. Gather up the
muslin and squeeze out as much of the coconut milk as possible. Discard the coconut from inside the cloth. Mix the
strained coconut milk with the liquid extracted from the whole
coconuts, then beat in all the remaining ingredients.

Place the mixture in a large saucepan and bring to the
boil. Lower the heat and simmer until the mixture thickens,
stirring constantly. Pour into a greased 20 cm/8 inch round
baking tin and bake for about 30 minutes until the top is
browned. Serve hot.

222 INDIAN FRUIT SALAD

Preparation time:
5 minutes, plus 3
hours soaking time

Cooking time:
20 minutes

Serves 4

Calories:
100 per portion

YOU WILL NEED:
225 g/8 oz dried tamarind
1 teaspoon chilli powder
sugar
2 green chillies, thinly sliced (optional)
1 x 2.5 cm/1 inch piece root ginger,
peeled and cut into fine strips
1 each pear, apple and banana or guava,
mango and any other fruit, cut into
small pieces

Put the tamarind in a bowl, cover with boiling water and set
aside for 3 hours or overnight.

Tip the tamarind and water into a sieve placed over a
saucepan and, using your fingers, push through as much pulp
as possible. Discard the husk and seeds.

Add the chilli powder, sugar to taste and simmer gently
for 15-20 minutes. Pour into a bowl and set aside to cool.

Stir in the chillies. (For a savoury accompaniment use
ginger and fruit.) Cover and chill before serving.

■ COOK'S TIP

*If decorating desserts as
shown, ensure that you wash
the fresh flowers and pat
them dry on absorbent
kitchen paper first.*

■ COOK'S TIP

*Use any fruit you like for this
dish, but those suggested here
are particularly well suited as
they absorb flavours readily.
The salad can also be served
with a savoury meal.*

223 SPICED SEMOLINA DESSERT

Preparation time:
5 minutes, plus
cooling time

Cooking time:
1 hour 10 minutes

Serves 4

Calories:
960 per portion

YOU WILL NEED:
225 g/8 oz semolina
4 tablespoons desiccated coconut
450 g/1 lb sugar
1 tablespoon poppy seeds
seeds of 6 cardamoms
600 ml/1 pint water
100 g/4 oz ghee, melted

Place the semolina in a large pan with the coconut, sugar, poppy and cardamom seeds. Mix well, then stir in the water. Bring to the boil, stirring constantly, then lower the heat and simmer for at least 1 hour, stirring frequently, until every ingredient is soft. Gradually add the ghee and mix well.

Transfer the mixture to a shallow tray and spread evenly. Leave to cool, then cut into triangles or diamond shapes. Store in an airtight container in a cool place.

224 WALNUT SWEET

Preparation time:
about 15 minutes,
including soaking time

Cooking time:
5-10 minutes

Serves 4-6

Calories:
500-350 per portion

YOU WILL NEED:
100 g/4 oz shelled walnuts
3 tablespoons oil
75 g/3 oz dates, stoned
900 ml/1 ½ pints water
150 g/5 oz sugar
40 g/1 ½ oz ground rice
3 tablespoons milk
apple flower, to decorate

Soak the walnuts in boiling water for 10 minutes, drain and remove the skins; dry on absorbent kitchen paper.

Heat the oil in a wok or deep frying pan, add the walnuts and fry quickly until lightly browned (take care not to burn them). Drain on absorbent kitchen paper.

Grind the nuts and dates in a blender, food processor or fine mincer. Bring the water to the boil and stir in the nut mixture and sugar. Blend the ground rice with the milk and add to the nut mixture. Bring back to the boil, stirring, and cook for 2 minutes until thickened.

Spoon into a warmed serving dish, decorate with an apple flower and serve hot.

COOK'S TIP

Known as Halwa, this is akin to the Middle Eastern halva and is good served as an after-dinner sweetmeat.

COOK'S TIP

To make an apple flower, thinly pare the rind from a small apple, taking care to keep it in one piece. Tightly curl the skin into a circle to make a flower shape.

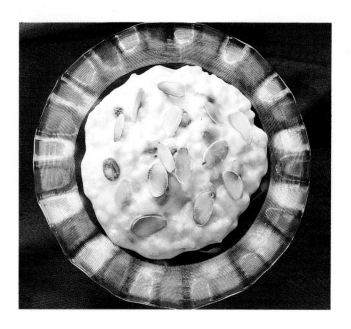

225 KHEER

Preparation time:
5 minutes, plus
cooling time

Cooking time:
1-1¼ hours

Serves 4

Calories:
490 per portion

YOU WILL NEED:
75 g/3 oz long-grain rice
1.8 litres/3 pints milk
50 g/2 oz sultanas
caster sugar
150 ml/¼ pint single cream
flaked almonds, to decorate

Put the rice and 1 litre/1¾ pints of the milk in a heavy-based pan. Cook gently at simmering point for 45-60 minutes, until most of the milk has been absorbed.

Add the remaining milk and sultanas, stir well and continue simmering until thickened. Remove from the heat and stir in sugar to taste.

Leave until completely cold, stirring occasionally to prevent a skin from forming, then stir in the cream.

Turn the mixture into small dishes and serve cold, sprinkled with flaked almonds.

226 BESSAN BARFI

Preparation time:
15 minutes

Cooking time:
25-30 minutes

Serves 4-6

Calories:
1,260-840 per portion

YOU WILL NEED:
350 g/12 oz unsalted butter or ghee
275 g/10 oz bessan flour, sifted
300 ml/½ pint water
350 g/12 oz sugar
a pinch of salt
10 small green cardamoms, shelled and seeds ground
30 g/1¼ oz mixed unsalted nuts, sliced (almonds, pistachio and cashew nuts for example)

Grease a 20 x 25 cm/8 x 10 inch baking dish. Using a non-stick or heavy-based pan, melt the butter or ghee and fry the bessan flour for 5-6 minutes, stirring constantly, until lightly browned. Remove from the heat.

Prepare a thick sugar syrup by placing the water in a pan with the sugar. Heat until the sugar dissolves, then bring to the boil for 5 minutes until the syrup is light golden and has thickened. If a small spoonful is taken out and cooled slightly it should form a single strand between your finger and thumb. If the syrup becomes too thick, add a little water.

Add the fried bessan to the syrup and cook on a low heat for 10-15 minutes, stirring constantly, until the mixture comes away from the sides of the pan and forms a ball. Remove from the heat, stir in the salt, ground cardamom and nuts. Pour into the greased dish and smooth the surface with a wet spatula. Cool and cut into cubes or diamond shapes.

■ COOK'S TIP

A kheer is the most popular sweet dish in India. If you like, add 3-4 drops rose water when the kheer has cooled, before decorating with the almonds.

■ COOK'S TIP

It is important to use a non-stick or heavy frying pan when making this chick pea flour fudge because bessan flour burns easily.

227 INDIAN ICE CREAM WITH PISTACHIOS

Preparation time:
10 minutes, plus 3-4
hours freezing time

Cooking time:
45 minutes

Serves 6-8

Calories:
370-280 per portion

YOU WILL NEED:
300 ml/½ pint double cream
300 ml/½ pint milk
1 x 400 g/14 oz can condensed milk
1 tablespoon clear honey
2 tablespoons chopped pistachios
2 teaspoons rose water
green food colouring (optional)

Heat the cream, milk, condensed milk and honey together in a heavy-based pan. Bring gently to the boil, stirring constantly, then simmer for 45 minutes over a very low heat. Remove from the heat, sprinkle in the pistachios and rose water, then add a little food colouring if liked. Allow to cool.

Pour the mixture into a shallow 900 ml/1½ pint freezer container or 6-8 kulfi moulds and freeze for 3-4 hours. Remove from the freezer and leave to stand at room temperature for 20-30 minutes to soften.

To serve, turn out the kulfi moulds (see Cook's Tip) or cut into squares.

228 COCONUT ICE CREAM

Preparation time:
15 minutes, plus 2-3
hours freezing time

Cooking time:
15-20 minutes

**Makes about 900
ml/1½ pints**

Total calories:
2,090

YOU WILL NEED:
350 ml/12 fl oz milk
75 g/3 oz desiccated coconut
350 ml/12 fl oz single cream
2 eggs
2 egg yolks
100 g/4 oz sugar
¼ teaspoon salt

Scald the milk, coconut and cream in a heavy-based pan over a low heat – about 15-20 minutes. Push through a fine sieve, pressing out as much of the coconut juice as possible. Discard the coconut.

Beat the eggs and egg yolks, sugar and salt with an electric beater until thick and mousse-like. Place over a pan of simmering water, stir in some of the coconut cream mixture, then the remainder and cook until the mixture will coat the back of a spoon. Cool quickly, then pour into freezer trays and freeze until mushy. Beat again to break up the ice crystals, return to the freezer trays and freeze until firm, about 2-3 hours, depending on freezer temperature and tray size.

Scoop into chilled glasses to serve.

▨ COOK'S TIP

To turn out ice creams, jellies and mousses from their moulds, dip the mould into a bowl of hot water for a couple of seconds, cover the mould with a plate and invert both plate and mould. Shake gently to release the contents, and then carefully lift off the mould.

▨ COOK'S TIP

Take the ice cream from the refrigerator about 30 minutes before serving – this helps to soften the ice cream so that it is easy to scoop.

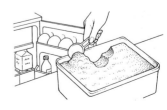

229 SPICED FRUIT SALAD

Preparation time:
10 minutes, plus 2
hours cooling time

Serves 4

Calories:
130 per portion

YOU WILL NEED:
2 oranges
2 pears
1 eating apple
2 guavas
2 bananas
juice of 1 lemon
1 teaspoon ground ginger
1 teaspoon garam masala
½ teaspoon freshly ground black pepper
salt

Peel the oranges and divide into segments, removing all the pith and pips. Peel and quarter the pears and apple, then cut them into thick slices. Peel the guavas and cut into chunky slices, including the seeds. Peel the bananas and slice thinly.

Place the fruit in a serving bowl and sprinkle over the lemon juice. Mix together the spices and salt, then sprinkle over the fruit. Fold very gently until each piece of fruit is coated in the lemon and spice mixture, then cover tightly and chill in the refrigerator for about 2 hours before serving.

230 CREAM CHEESE BALLS IN SYRUP

Preparation time:
15 minutes, plus
making panir

Cooking time:
2¼ hours

Makes 12-15

Calories:
400 per ball

YOU WILL NEED:
1 recipe Panir (see Cook's Tip)
75 g/3 oz blanched almonds, chopped
115 g/4½ oz semolina
12-15 cubes sugar
FOR THE SYRUP
1 litre/1¾ pints water
200 g/8 oz sugar
pinch of cream of tartar
½ teaspoon rose water

Stir the panir to a smooth paste, then add the almonds and semolina. Knead well until smooth.

When the palm of the hand is greasy, mould the paste. Break the dough into 12-15 pieces, about the size of walnuts. Shape into balls, moulding each one around a sugar cube.

To make the syrup, put all the ingredients except the rose water in a heavy-based pan and heat gently until the sugar dissolves. Bring to the boil, add the balls of dough, then lower the heat and simmer very gently for 2 hours. Stir in the rose water, then serve hot or cold.

▨ COOK'S TIP

Known in India as chaat, this dish is sometimes served as an appetizer or accompaniment to hot main-course curries.

▨ COOK'S TIP

For panir, bring 2.4 litres/ 4 pints milk to the boil. Let cool to 37C/98F. Beat in 500 ml/17 fl oz natural yogurt, 4 teaspoons lemon juice and 1 tablespoon salt.

Leave in a warm place 12 hours. Strain through muslin for 30 minutes, then squeeze out the liquid. Shape in the cloth and place under a weight 3 hours.

231 CARROT PUDDING

Preparation time:
5 minutes

Cooking time:
about 55 minutes

Serves 4

Calories:
530 per portion

YOU WILL NEED:
450 g/1 lb carrots, grated
225 g/8 oz sugar
1.5 litres/2 ½ pints milk
6 cardamoms
1 tablespoon sultanas
1 tablespoon slivered almonds

Put the carrots in a bowl and sprinkle with the sugar. Set aside.

Put the milk in a large pan with the cardamoms. Bring to the boil and boil steadily for 45 minutes or until the milk is reduced by half. Add the carrot and sugar mixture and simmer until the mixture thickens. Remove the pan from the heat, leave to cool slightly, then stir in the sultanas and almonds. Serve hot or cold.

232 EIGHT-JEWEL RICE PUDDING

Preparation time:
20 minutes

Cooking time:
1¼-1½ hours

Serves 6

Calories:
550 per portion

YOU WILL NEED:
350 g/12 oz pudding rice
4 tablespoons caster sugar
50 g/2 oz unsalted butter
100 g/4 oz glacé cherries, chopped
50 g/2 oz crystallized orange peel, chopped
25 g/1 oz each angelica, walnuts and blanched almonds, chopped
50 g/2 oz seedless raisins, chopped
5 tablespoons sweet red bean paste
FOR THE SYRUP
(see Cook's Tip)

Rinse the rice, drain and put in a pan with enough water to cover. Simmer for 15 minutes; drain. Stir in the sugar and half the butter.

Use the remaining butter to grease a 900 ml/1½ pint pudding basin, then line with a thin layer of rice. Press a little of each fruit and nut into this to make a decorative pattern. Mix the remaining rice, fruit and nuts. Spoon alternate layers of this rice mixture and bean paste into the basin finishing with a layer of rice. Press down firmly. Cover with greaseproof paper and pleated foil and steam for 1-1¼ hours.

Turn the pudding out on to a serving dish and serve hot with the warm syrup.

■ COOK'S TIP

This unusual pudding, known as Gajjar Kheer in India, is very rich and sweet and perfect to serve after a light lunch.

■ COOK'S TIP

To make the syrup for this recipe, bring 300 ml/½ pint water mixed with 50 g/2 oz sugar to the boil, stirring constantly. Remove from the heat and add a few drops of *almond essence, vanilla essence, rose water or orange water. Pour over the pudding and serve hot.*

233 DOUGHNUT SPIRALS IN SYRUP

Preparation time:
15 minutes, plus
overnight standing

Cooking time:
about 10 minutes

Makes 20-24

Calories:
270 per spiral

YOU WILL NEED:
275 g/10 oz plain flour
40 g/1 ½ oz rice flour
pinch of baking powder
½ teaspoon salt
175 ml/6 fl oz water
vegetable oil for deep frying
FOR THE SYRUP
1 litre/1 ¾ pints water
200 g/8 oz sugar
pinch of cream of tartar
½ teaspoon rose water
*½ teaspoon yellow or red food colouring
(optional)*

Sift the flours, baking powder and salt into a bowl. Gradually add the water and beat to a smooth batter. Cover and chill overnight.

To make the syrup, put the water, sugar and cream of tartar in a heavy-based pan and heat to dissolve the sugar. Add the rose water and food colouring if used.

Heat the oil, put the batter in a piping bag fitted with a large plain nozzle and pipe spirals, about 10 cm/4 inches in diameter, into the hot oil. Deep fry for about 3 minutes until crisp, then drain on absorbent kitchen paper.

Immerse the spirals in the syrup for 30 seconds while still warm. Serve warm or cold.

234 SEMOLINA BARFI

Preparation time:
10 minutes, plus
cooling time

Cooking time:
about 20 minutes

Serves 4-6

Calories:
470-310 per portion

YOU WILL NEED:
50 g/2 oz fine semolina
100 g/4 oz sugar
450 ml/¾ pint milk
50 g/2 oz butter
10 cardamoms, crushed
*75 g/3 oz blanched almonds, halved and
toasted*

Place the semolina and sugar in a heavy-based pan and stir in the milk gradually until smooth. Add the butter in small pieces. Bring to the boil, stirring, then simmer for 3-4 minutes, until thickened, stirring occasionally to prevent sticking. Add the crushed cardamoms and continue cooking for another 10 minutes or until the mixture leaves the sides of the pan.

Spread on a buttered plate or dish to a thickness of 1 to 1.5 cm/½ to 1 inch. Leave until almost cold and then decorate with the almonds. Serve cold, cut into slices or squares.

▣ COOK'S TIP

*To ring the changes, try using
kewra water or essence
instead of rose water, or
colour the spirals with
1 teaspoon jalebi powder
or powdered turmeric.*

▣ COOK'S TIP

*Semolina can be used in
savoury dishes as well as in
sweet puddings, cakes and
biscuits. These sweets can be
served after a meal, but make
a lovely gift, too.*

235 CARROT HALWA

Preparation time:
10 minutes

Cooking time:
25-30 minutes

Serves 4-6

Calories:
520-350 per portion

YOU WILL NEED:
1.2 litres/2 pints milk
225 g/8 oz carrots, finely grated
75 g/3 oz butter
1 tablespoon golden syrup
100 g/4 oz sugar
50 g/2 oz sultanas or raisins
1 teaspoon cardamom seeds, crushed

Place the milk and carrots in a heavy-based pan and cook over a high heat, stirring occasionally, until the liquid has evaporated.

Add the butter, syrup, sugar and fruit. Stir until the butter and sugar have melted, then cook for 15-20 minutes, stirring frequently, until the mixture starts to leave the sides of the pan.

Pour into a shallow buttered dish and spread evenly. Sprinkle with the crushed cardamoms. Cut into slices and serve warm or cold.

236 ALMOND BARFI

Preparation time:
5 minutes

Cooking time:
50 minutes

Serves 4

Calories:
240 per portion

YOU WILL NEED:
750 ml/1 ¼ pints milk
50 g/2 oz caster sugar
50 g/2 oz ground almonds
6 cardamom seeds, peeled and crushed

Put the milk in a large saucepan and heat for about 45 minutes until it is reduced to a thick, lumpy consistency. Stir occasionally and be careful not to let the milk burn.

When it is thick and lumpy, stir in the sugar, then add the almonds and cook for 2 minutes. Spread on a buttered plate and sprinkle with the crushed cardamom. Serve warm, cut into wedges or diamond shapes.

■ COOK'S TIP

Syrup won't trail everywhere if you continually turn the spoon over as you take it from the tin and add it to the pan.

■ COOK'S TIP

If you like it, add a couple of drops of almond essence to the mixture for an extra strong almond flavour.